Enabling Children's Learning
Through Drawing

For Dawn
with love

Enabling Children's Learning Through Drawing

Fred Sedgwick

David Fulton Publishers

London

David Fulton Publishers Ltd
Ormond House, 26–27 Boswell Street, London WC1N 3JZ
www.fultonpublishers.co.uk

First published in Great Britain by David Fulton Publishers in 2002

Note: The right of Fred Sedgwick to be identified as the author of this work has been asserted by him in accordance with the Copyright, Designs and Patents Act 1988.

Copyright © Fred Sedgwick 2002

British Library Cataloguing in Publication Data
A catalogue record for this book is available from the British Library.

ISBN 1–85346–836–3

Typeset by Patrick Armstrong, Book Production Services, London
Printed in Great Britain by Bell and Bain Ltd, Glasgow

Contents

Look

harder than you thought possible
at whorl   arch   loop
the frail architecture
of a bird's skull's emptiness
at stamen   pistil   leaf
or here   under glass
at this decaying wasp's
velvet rugby strip
its india-paper wings

Now set your pencil free
to work in a thousand ways
and you'll find words
shaping up in your mind

Lay them roughly down
alongside your sketches
Between scribbles
and ways of making lines
some you're insisting wrong
wriggles a kind of truth
harder than you thought possible
                              [F.S.]
It will serve for the time being

We have learned that drawing is cool
                    Henry (10 years)

Acknowledgements

I am grateful to the staff and children at Bealings Primary School, Suffolk. My special thanks go to Duncan Bathgate and Pam Fletcher. Thanks also to Melissa Page at St Nicholas School, Letchworth, Herts; Kim Kelway and her staff at Gislingham School, Suffolk; and to Kath Cook and her staff at Middleton School, Suffolk. I am grateful for comments on early drafts of this book from Duncan Bathgate, Dawn Sedgwick and Andrea Durrant. All crudities of thought or expression, though, are my own, and probably the result of not taking their advice. Thanks, once again, to Henry Burns Elliot and Emily Roeves, in spite of everything.

Introduction

Here is a cornerstone to lay with the very foundations of all teaching. I suggest that students lay it, if they can, before they try, consciously, to teach anything (we are teaching something *un*consciously most of the time when we talk to others). I wish someone had told me about it when I started teaching in the late sixties:

A teacher who is not learning is not teaching.

The teacher may be doing two other things. First, she may be training, which means pushing students along tracks like a shunting engine, or pulling them like an express. Someone else has laid these tracks, probably with statutory powers, insisting that this is the route that the students should take. Nowadays, teachers have to tell their students facts that these powers insist the children should know. These facts are often trivia, such as the phonemes, thin poems and shape poems in the Literacy Strategy. Teaching these facts requires no prior, simultaneous or later learning on the part of the teacher. It is not education – it is training.

Second, the teacher may be preaching. This is another, though not entirely unrelated matter. She may be preaching the educational orthodoxies of the time, which are also political orthodoxies. She may be preaching some religious orthodoxies as well and there is an increasing number of examples of this.

News on the radio from Northern Ireland, as I write, colours these comments, so to speak. Orange Loyalists protest with abuse, whistles, horns and bricks at four- and five-year-old children walking to school at Holy Cross Primary in Belfast (green, of course). If this is a surprising reference in a book about learning and drawing, I believe that no teacher – and no learner – works in a politics-free context. Throughout this book, I try to place what I do with the children in the everyday context; sometimes overtly political (as in Belfast), sometimes less obviously political, for example the attempt at control over the minds of teachers and children that the current National Curriculum represents.

Conventionally, the position of the preacher is that of someone who has no need to learn, at least in her role as a preacher. This person has sorted things out. The maps are fully charted. She knows what needs to be known, and is now telling the congregation what she knows; the congregation must also know it soon if it wants to be saved. This is not an educational position and will not succeed in teaching anyone anything.

In contrast to both the trainer and the preacher, the teacher must be a learner. Writers have to learn all the time too. We are concerned with education. If I believe, when I enter a school, that I know everything there is to be known about what I am going to teach, I will not only be selling the students short. I am selling myself short, too. I do not simply mean that the children will say interesting things that I can write down for future use, or that teachers will give me useful tips for my own work in other schools. I mean that I should be, temporarily, a member of a community of scholars learning alongside everyone else in that place; about what they are learning, and about them. About what it is to be human. All writers know this, unless they are concerned only with raising a laugh, or a thrill, or in stimulating false emotions. Writers are learners: novelists explore the human condition, and poets explore that condition also, but go beneath it as far as they can, as far as they dare.

The pregnant horse in the Pileta caves

As a writer about education, I have learned a lesson from prehistory. In the Pileta caves near Ronda in southern Spain, there are drawings on a rock wall. My favourite represents a pregnant horse rearing on her hind legs. Some man, some woman (some child perhaps!) drew her over 4,000 years ago – two millennia before the angels sang on the hillside outside Bethlehem – or so the young Spanish student guide tells us (in Spanish, Italian, French, German and English – shaming us British monoglots). The artist used an ochre that looks now like dried blood. There is also a giant fish in charcoal-like black-grey on light grey, drawn with magisterial sweeps of whatever graphic tool the artist had found. Then there are tiny sudden movements high up. *Fledermaus! Pipistrello! Chauves-souris! Murcielago!* Delighted cries fill the cave: modern Europeans united, sighting a creature that has been here as long as the drawings. Look! A bat! I say to my son, in blunt English.

Every time I visit the caves – with their stalagmites and stalactites, the drip of limestone, one inch every 1,000 years – I marvel at these pictures, seen, as they are, by the light of the gas lamps that package tourists have to carry along the slippery floors. I love them, first, because they are beautiful. The proportions feel right, the drawing looks assured, the colours are weathered (or rather, unweathered) by 4,000 years or more of an atmosphere it is difficult and frightening to think about. I love them, too, because no one will ever own them. The idea that any person should possess someone else's attempt to understand the world, and then, because of her economic power, should be able to hang it on her walls where no one else can see it, seems to me to be perverse. I write this, despite the fact that over a period of 20 years, in a necessarily small way, we have bought pictures and carvings for our house. As Walt Whitman wrote, 'Do I contradict myself? / Very well then I contradict myself, / I am large, I contain multitudes.'

I love these images, secondly, because of a conviction that those ancient artists were doing two important things. They were learning, and they were communicating. They were learning about, and communicating with, themselves. They were learning about, and communicating with, each other. As I stand in front of them, they communicate with me. And I learn, not only about them, but also

2

about what drawing is. I also learn something about myself, and something about what it is to be a human being.

It is impossible to say what those makers were learning, or what they were telling each other. It may have been practical (we have killed and can eat, we must kill in order to eat). It may have been purely to give pleasure (Look at this! I have done it! Do you like it?). It may have been religious: the fish may have spiritual significance, as later fish did in the catacombs in Rome, standing secretly for the presence of worshippers of Christ. Speculation on this will always be as educational and interesting as it is useless.

> Some American Indian tribes do not have a word in their vocabulary for 'art', yet their cultures overflow with paintings, drawings, sculpture and models, weaving, pattern-making and decoration. It is so much a part of their needs and style that it seems to become as unselfconscious as breathing. (Morgan 1988: 1)

She suggests that this need is true of children. I am sure that it is also true of the ancient dwellers in the caves at Pileta.

Looking at children's drawings in the light of those ancient ones helps us to understand both children and drawing. Goethe wrote that anyone who tries to live in the present without taking sustenance from the past is living from hand to mouth. Many things from human history sustain us. Those of us who are people of the book – Jews, Muslims, Christians – are sustained by religious writings: myths, poetry, prophesy, genealogy, epistles, epic, gospel. We are also sustained by philosophy, the poetry of Shakespeare ('Poor soul, the centre of my sinful earth'), the paintings and drawings of Leonardo da Vinci, the music of Mozart and Bach and Louis Armstrong. There are less obvious things, too, such as these eternal drawings among stalagmites, stalactites, and careering bats in an obscure cave in Spain. And there are the languages that the human race uses to name them.

And deep down here, in the dark cave, right now, are my notes.

The goose's foot

Leonardo da Vinci is another inspiration behind this book. I don't mean his great religious paintings, much as I admire their grandeur (widely recognised) and their subversiveness (less widely appreciated): Mary apparently already pregnant in *The Annunciation*; the frightening face of St Anne in the famous cartoon; the gesture of St John, his index finger sticking ambiguously upwards. I mean the teeming mirror-written jottings and sketches that he made all over notebooks in order to further his understanding of, it appears, almost anything. In Jean Mathe's *Leonardo's Inventions* (1980), for example, page after page is covered with exploratory writing and drawing of all kinds of artifacts. I leaf through and choose at random: a water pump, a dredger, a snorkel, a flying machine, cogwheels and gearwheels. Or I look at Martin Clayton's *Leonardo da Vinci: the Anatomy of Man* (1992), and find a foetus, imagined (obviously); the liver, the spleen, the alimentary tract and the 'hydrostatics of the bladder'.

The flavour of Leonardo's notes, of his passionate will to know, is clear in this passage:

> Observe the goose's foot: if it were always open or always closed the creature would not be able to make any kind of movement. While with the curve of the foot outwards it has more perception of the water in going forward than the foot would have as it is drawn back … (Richter 1980: 95)

Were he alive today, Leonardo would watch with fascination and desire to learn, if they are not the same things, a man getting into his car:

> He stands for a moment by the shiny door. Then, with his right hand, he clicks down the lever, and pulls the door open. Before it is half-open, he has lifted his left leg, and he then places it in the well, meanwhile bending his body into a half sitting position. He then sits, and pulls in his right leg, almost simultaneously pulling the door shut. His right hand turns clockwise some 35 degrees …

Here is a suggested exercise that would be interesting for both teachers and children. Draw, and write about, an ordinary thing happening. A man making tea; a toddler kicking or throwing a ball; a barmaid or barman pulling a pint; a woman weeding a garden; a man opening a flat Perspex box and putting a CD on the player; a child untying bows, pulling apart wrapping paper and opening a present on a birthday; a woman (my neighbour, as it happens) lifting her child over my fence and placing him in my arms so that he can feed my rabbit …

Like early humankind in the Pileta caves and like Leonardo, children have a need to communicate. Often they are unconsciously informing us (though they are informing themselves first) of some need, some joy, some desire (see the drawings in this book). More obviously, they have a need to learn. Children are desperate that they should not misunderstand the circumstances in which they find themselves. I still find myself momentarily infuriated by an article I read some years ago in which a teacher prattled facetiously about the difficult task of instilling into his charges some enthusiasm for knowledge. Children want to learn. Watch toddlers exploring a drain cover; or carrying mud in spades and buckets around a wet winter garden, building dams; or examining the belly of a tortoise with the help of a mirror under it – all images I am familiar with. It is easy, if we are attentive, to find evidence of this desperation to learn in the drawings in this book.

Above all, whether they know it or not, children drawing are communicating with themselves. I have watched them doing this, their lips moving as they study, with their brows furrowed in concentration, both on their drawings, and the subject of their drawings. They look entranced. I feel entranced, looking at them.

A further point: marks – such as those on the rock walls of the Pileta caves, in Leonardo's notebooks, in children's notebooks – have to be made before they can be interpreted. The making of a mark precedes the interpretation of it. This should alert us to the fact that children, like early humankind, are makers of marks before they are interpreters of them. If this seems obvious, it is worth asking why, with our arguments about phonics and reading schemes, we implicitly conceive of children as beings who have to learn to interpret marks before we take much interest in the marks they make. This almost universal practice is a misunderstanding: children are writers and drawers before they are readers and critics. Let us study children's early marks – whether they are scribbles on the wall, or drawings consciously made with a view to creating art – with this understanding: their mark-making, and our sensitive understanding of it, will make them better readers and better writers, and us better teachers. And it will, come to that, make us better readers and writers too.

Leonardo's learning, the cave dwellers' learning, the children's learning … I am also writing about my learning. Or, more accurately, I am writing in order to learn, much as I believe the people listed above are drawing to learn. I see this book from where I am now – at the beginning of it – as a research project, and I remember something I have written before that I need again. It is this: every poem, every dance, every painting, every drawing, is a research project into the relationship into the differences between myself and the rest of the world. Because I am doing research, I hope that what I understand about children and their drawing will be different when I have sent my final draft to the publisher from my current understanding. Confident as I am in what I believe about children and drawing, I am not so arrogant as to think that the children cannot teach me more.

The children who I hope will teach me work in a primary school in Suffolk called Bealings.

Bealings Primary School

I chose this village school for my project for five reasons. First, it is close to my home. Second, the head teacher, Duncan Bathgate, is a friend of mine. Third, the teachers want to expand their practice, rather than limit it to current (and, certainly, temporary) statutory requirements. Fourth, I know the children and they know me. Fifth, Bealings is a good school.

I need, of course, to expand on my final reason for choosing this school. It is a school with committed aesthetic and progressive values. Children do not compete with each other for WELL DONE stickers, or house points, or stars on a chart in the classroom. The atmosphere is something like a community of scholars, where everyone, including Duncan, is a learner. The children have liberties not seen in all schools: they move freely around. They are not regimented on the playground at the end of playtime. The adults listen to them. Parents are welcome in lessons and play a large part in the running of the school. Also, Bealings has weathered the storm of OFSTED. Neither the progressive quality of the school, nor the fact that it has impressed OFSTED need surprise us much: it is the combination of the two that is startling. OFSTED, and the rest of the teacher-control apparatus that has been built by successive governments over the past 20 years, tends to favour data-driven evaluations. How good are the SATs results? Where is the school in the league tables? And this makes schools competitive, both with each other and in their approach to children's progress. Schools with humane values that receive good reports have one strong factor in common: a head teacher who knows what he stands for and is both courageous enough, and intellectually able, to stand up for his values.

The school serves a small village, but children come from nearby towns (Ipswich and Woodbridge) and other villages, sometimes from local private schools. It is approached up a narrow road past an elegant pub, the *Admiral's Head*. On one side of the road is the old HORSA hut (a relic of an old and largely forgotten government initiative, RSA stands for the Raising of the School-leaving Age) which now serves as a dining room. There is a small car park, and a field. On the other side is the main Victorian building containing a hall and three classrooms.

There is an arts garden in the school grounds. Pam Fletcher is the deputy head of Bealings Primary School, and I have drawn on her notes on the application form for a grant from Artworks (the National Children's Art Awards) to write this next passage about the current state of the garden.

Twenty pupils went on a study trip to St Ives in Cornwall. They stayed at a hotel a few yards from the twin nerve centres of the town: Barbara Hepworth's house with its studio and garden, and the Tate Gallery. Subsequently, 50 eight- to eleven-year-olds made sculptures at school. They had intended to study the paintings of Ben Nicholson and Alfred Wallis. But because everyone was so impressed by the sculpture garden outside Barbara Hepworth's house, this became the main focus of the project (see Hepworth 1985 for marvellous images of this place).

I was pleased that the school had chosen this focus, because I love the place. I visited the Hepworth studio and garden some years ago. The smooth abstract sculptures seem to grow out of the grass behind the powerful leaves of exotic plants. It is a kind of paradox that, although they are abstract, these sculptures celebrate humanity. The trees create an open room with, on a good summer's day, a 'blue true dream of sky' as its ceiling. It is exhilarating to look at nature through Hepworth's abstracts. I have felt this ever since my friend, the poet John Cotton, photographed my eight-year-old son with my friend's Jack Russell terrier and myself in front of Hepworth's huge work at Snape Maltings (near Aldeburgh). Behind the art, the human beings and the dog is the huge Suffolk sky, seamed to the flat marshes. Weathered and, apparently, indestructible, the bronzes are, as Picasso said of his own pictures, timeless 'weapons of war against brutality and darkness'. They are parts from a piece called *The Family of Man* (see Curtis and Wilkinson 1994 for a fuller picture of this work).

In St Ives, the children from Bealings explored Hepworth's large outdoor work. One child wrote 'the garden has lots of wonderful sculptures … they all have holes in them! It is a wonderful place.' They also loved 'the workshop, full of hammers and half-completed statues, with her overalls still hanging up'. The children sat in the garden and looked and sketched from different angles. Adults and pupils touched the sculptures – a necessary privilege with statues, I would say, but one usually denied (for good reasons, I know, I know) in conventional galleries. They also photographed them.

When the children got back to Suffolk they made clay models of the sculptures, and painted pictures of them. They began to plan their own sculptures and their own garden. The pupils sketched and made clay maquettes. They made armatures of three sculptures from steel rods, hoops and chicken wire. They covered them with Modroc and cement render. Finally, they painted and varnished the sculptures. 'My favourite bit. The painting!' wrote one child. 'We put on loads of layers of paint and mixed lots of colours. Then we varnished them.' The end result was bronze and silver sculptures 'which won't get battered by the weather'.

Neither the pupils nor the teachers had worked on such a large scale before, nor had they worked with this medium. They modified initial plans as they came across constraints and new possibilities. They worked with tenacity and concentration, even when things did not go to plan. They were highly motivated and, finally, proud of their achievements. They were able to make large 3D images and then set them into the school's environment. The children now have a love of sculpture, with the added benefit that there now exists a lasting resource for the school and the village.

These paragraphs (derived from Pam's notes) are interesting for four reasons. First, they show the teachers and children focusing progressively. This piece of jargon comes from educational research. As you look at the setting that you are studying, it emerges that what interested you as you began interests you less now, and something else has become what matters. For example, in the writing of an MA thesis, I discovered that I was not as concerned with head teachers and the way they hope to change schools as I had been at the beginning, and was more interested in how teachers change their own classrooms. For the Bealings children, it means that the travellers arrive in St Ives with a focus on the work of Alfred Wallis and Ben Nicholson; but, as they work, they become obsessed by a different one – the work of Barbara Hepworth. Not only is the initial focus educational (the Wallis and the Nicholson are not dismissed). Not only is the final focus interesting – it became an obsession. Crucially, the move from one to the other is educational too. Changing your mind is good exercise. It involves learning.

Second, the whole project had involved, as Duncan said, decision-making as the children's learning became more and more self-directed. Robin Tanner said that 'the arts above all other activities involve us in the subtle element of choice. Every creative act is an act of choosing ...' (1984, quoted in Morgan 1988). When I look back at this project, I see choices being offered and made almost all the time, and I reckon that makes it infinitely more educational than the limited training offered by the National Curriculum.

Third, the children seem to have no problem trying to understand and to enjoy modern art. While many adults look at non-figurative sculpture and, baffled and uncomprehending, turn away, children readily take up the challenge because they are untrammelled by the notion that art has to be photographic in character. I have their writing in front of me: 'her garden was beautiful, plants and sculptures with holes ... I couldn't wait to start building our own sculptures in the pond area at the back of the school ...' Many adults – most, probably – could learn from children's ways with modern art: their playful, joyous acceptance. This is in stark contrast to our responses, which, conventionally, range from benign bemusement to philistine hostility.

Fourth, the garden affects the whole community, the village of Bealings. There will be open days, says Duncan; but in the meantime locals cutting through the village on the pathway behind the church enjoy an elevated view of the sculpture garden with its pond, hazel tunnel and exotic plants. A new group of children will work in this area next summer, using it as preparatory work for the next visit to St Ives. That group will bring back responses, and so the garden will grow in unexpected ways. What Duncan calls this 'echoing back and forth between the two gardens' is central to the life of the project.

This is the school where I taught the drawings in this book. These children had looked, laid sketches roughly down, scribbled notes, made choices, and found a kind of truth that would serve them for the time being, perhaps for a lifetime, perhaps beyond. They showed me that, whatever one's stated purpose in making a given drawing, one is inevitably in the business of learning. This book is set in that context: learning, in the Pileta caves, in Leonardo's notebooks, in a school that takes the arts seriously. Therefore, it is not a book of tips for teachers. It is a case study of the teaching and learning of drawing in a particular place, and with certain inspirations. Other teachers will teach as well, or better, in other places and with other inspirations. This, though, is where I am.

Note

All but some of the face and cat drawings, and some of the drawings in Chapter 4, which were made on large paper, are reproduced at full size. Often when children leave white space around their images it is important, so the spaces are included too. To crop pictures, potentially at least, is to take meaning away.

1 Faces and Cats

The faces

I would like to write – I would like to believe – that line is everything. It would make things simple. Line is how we see things. It is also how we write things: all these letters, little curly lines themselves, arranged in words and then in lines, and those lines arranged again in even neater lines on my screen, on my printout, and eventually in this book. We separate our potential knowledge of the world – curricula – into subjects with lines: rather dubiously, it seems to me. In newspapers, lines separate stories from each other. Lines also supply other boundaries: between nations on the map, between religious and political beliefs.

But do we, in fact, perceive things visually, not in terms of lines, but in terms of the spaces between lines? I want to try an exercise in helping children to do this later on (the climbing frames, pp. 87–97). Paradoxically, this will make the children more certain in their perception of the lines of which the objects are, in commonsensical terms, made. Certainly, as I jot these words in the margins of my typescript on a summer evening in the garden, I am aware that if I look at the spaces between lines, or (more accurately) between the edges of things – leaves, for example – I am more aware of the things – the leaves – themselves. While discussing the illustration of children's books, Quentin Blake pointed out that the lines we see around things when we draw them do not exist. Spaces do.

Perhaps the notion of line is western European ethnocentric. In the Nigerian Yoruba culture, Emmanuel Jegede (the artist/poet/musician) once told me line is secondary to carving. It may be that some human beings perceive the world, not in terms of line at all, but in terms of depth. Maybe in western Europe we are too concerned with boundaries and edges, and not concerned enough with space, substance and density. But I am stuck with line, contentedly enough while I write this book, comforted by William Blake: 'The more distinct, sharp and wiry the bounding line, the more perfect the work of art ...' (quoted in Read 1931).

I began it on an untrustworthy spring morning. The light hinted at summer and the temperature hinted at winter. After much thought, after writing a long proposal, and after planning for some weeks with Duncan, I drove the five miles east out of town to Bealings Primary School. Duncan, Pam and their colleagues are creating a little arts centre here, both in the heart of and around the edges of their school.

10

One of Duncan's inspirations is obviously the Hepworth studio in St Ives, Cornwall – another is Kettle's Yard in Cambridge. This can best be described as an open house created by Jim Ede (one-time curator at the Tate Gallery) from almost-derelict cottages near St John's College. Its rationale – though neither its atmosphere nor the quality of what is on view – can be gleaned from the sentence 'Art [is] better approached in the intimate surroundings of a home' (Kettle's Yard 1995: 3). The house contains not just pictures and sculptures (by Gaudier-Brzeska, Hepworth and David Jones, among others) but also a collection of books, wall hangings, rugs, plants, furniture and pottery. When I try to capture the atmosphere of the house, I think of words such as 'organic'. The pieces seem to be growing in the place, cool and authentic, much as Hepworth's sculptures seem to be growing in her garden. Nothing is here merely for style, or for a thrill, or for a laugh. The house is both full of feeling, and empty of sentimentality. I rejoice in its human scale, and the evident fact that it is the home of a person who has become accustomed to look at natural objects – pebbles, for example, and shells, and wood – and to spend emotional and intellectual energy on that looking.

In Duncan's classroom (the children are aged nine, ten and eleven) there are fishing nets draped across a display of pictures and writing about the sea. There are buoys, huge waders, keepnets, and lamps. On another wall are poems written by some of the children following the study of *Romeo and Juliet* during one of my previous visits. On another wall are war poems, written after studying three or four of Wilfred Owen's poems, and a huge display of 'Our Images of War in the Style of Picasso' composed of visual quotations from Guernica. On another, there are imitations of Yoruba poems about twins. Like many Nigerians, Emmanuel Jegede is a twin, and the mythology surrounding that strange phenomenon fascinates me, and, using his poems, I have passed some of this fascination on to these children.

In Duncan's spacious study (spacious, that is, for a school of only 90 pupils) there is a large, low, square, wooden table in the middle. His neat desk is pushed to one wall. Dried plants as tall as me firework out of ceramic pots in two corners of the room. There is an eclectic collection of recent books about teaching. He had, he told me, given each teacher a budget to buy books that appealed to them. The usual statutory files, from central government and from the local authority, look neat and undisturbed in one corner. I disturb one. *Moving Language Forward* (or something like that) is depressingly mechanistic. It is full of tables representing levels, and the only children's writing that I can see are letters, or that weak, problematic genre foisted on children these days by successive governments, 'writing to persuade'. On the walls of the room are examples of children's work – imitations of Modigliani, for example – and reproductions of modern art.

Duncan enthused about a future project involving visiting poets, artists and dancers. He can afford this project (and this enthusiasm) because Bealings is now 'a beacon school', and will be receiving money to finance such initiatives. Other schools in the county that are – according to inspections, test results, league tables and the like – less successful than Bealings will be involved in the project.

I asked the seven-, eight- and nine-year-old children to draw friends' faces. Drawing is an important way (conventionally underrated by managers in education, i.e. politicians, advisers and inspectors) in which we can rediscover, almost at will, the world in which we live. Even more importantly, as we draw, we build a bridge between ourselves and our world. Thus drawing strengthens our position in the world, and our grip on that world.

Not teaching the faces

Here are three examples, by Anna, Rosemary and Lindsay (Figures 1.1, 1.2 and 1.3). These drawings are ordinary. Similar work can be found in decent schools all over the country. These pictures were done without any teaching, or more accurately, they were done without any teaching immediately before the children worked. The school's tradition of teaching art is strong, as I have shown, and that tradition obviously informed what the children did on this occasion. There had been, so to speak, long-term teaching: witness the relationship with St Ives and the resultant gardens and the sculptures. But there had been no short-term teaching. The deliberate avoidance of teaching on that morning (not, I found, easy to do) reminded me of an orthodoxy among some teachers 20 years ago. Teachers should not teach, but be 'enablers of learning'. They should 'provide an environment that helps children to discover for themselves what they need to know when they are ready for it'. I understood then – and understand now – the motivation for such thinking. It aimed at offering an education that set the children free to discover their world and their relationship to it. But it neglected how much the teacher has to do in both talking and listening to the children. I appreciate now that this notion can be seen as a sentimental evasion of responsibility.

With these children I took the no-teaching rule literally: 'Just draw your friend's face.' It was so far from teaching that it was merely instruction, or even the giving of an order (although that, I know, is not what the sixties progressives meant). I let the children do what they wanted: they drew tentatively, then rubbed lines out, feverishly, as though the rubbing out meant more that the lines themselves. I let them, if they wanted, cover no more than the corner of their sheets of A4 paper. I didn't interrupt them with requests that they 'look harder', and I didn't worry them with suggestions about how they might get their pencils to make different kinds of mark.

Anna's drawing (Figure 1.1) has attempts at accuracy in it, but is static and dull. Rosemary's drawing (Figure 1.2) is the smallest of the drawings, and more interesting than the other two: a hint of the cartoon (Posy Simmonds' dowdier women, in *Guardian* strips perhaps?) lurks in there somewhere. Lindsay's drawing (Figure 1.3) had life from the beginning, partly because she noticed that Hannah was looking at her in order to draw her. Hence that sidelong glance: the girls were sitting side by side.

Teaching the faces

I then taught the children in an old-fashioned instructional way. I give here the notes of my lesson (in bold type as these four rules constitute the basic building blocks of this book).

1.1

1.2

1.3

1. **no erasers**
2. **close-up**
3. **making different kinds of pencil mark**
4. **look look look (quote Blake and Tardios)**

I had taught in this way many times before and those bare notes were all I needed. Expanded they look like this, much like notes I prepared on my first teaching practice 30-odd years ago. They are merely notes to myself but expanded to include objectives. Objectives post-dated my college days and I came to distrust them. This is because to focus on the future, on what children might achieve one day, is to play down first, what they are now, and second, the teacher's creativity. But I include them because they are now part of the everyday currency of teaching.

Teaching objectives
1. To help the children to look closely
2. To help them to transfer the results of their looking to their drawing
3. To help them to learn about the appearance and structure of the human face
4. To help them make a work of art

Process of the lesson
The children may not use erasers. Point out the importance of keeping 'first thoughts', as in drawings by Giacometti and others. Tell the children that 'wrong lines might come is useful later – please leave them there and then do the right line, or even another line that seems even more right'.

Ask the children to draw subjects 'close-up'. Tell them little tiny images in the corner of the paper won't be much help. 'Perhaps you could draw your subject so close-up that it won't fit on the page. I want your drawings done so that I can see the details.' Don't just say you want 'big drawings'.

Ask the children to work on the kinds of mark a pencil can make. Give them scraps of paper and ask them to make as many different kinds of mark as they can think of. This exercise 'will guarantee' (as Margaret Morgan, one-time art adviser in Suffolk, used to say) 'to raise the standards of drawing in your school – overnight'. There is a problem here because, for the child, the scribble is associated with the opposite of order and control: it is usually done as a result of strong emotion, or to rub something out. In this exercise, scribbling has a very different function that, probably, only the teacher will understand.

Ask the children to look 'until it hurts' (Blake's phrase). As the poet George Tardios wrote: 'The world is troubled / With a lack of looking' (quoted in Pirrie 1987). A wonderful quotation that the art educationalist Andrea Durrant gave me adds strength to this:

It is in order to really see, to see ever deeper, even more intensely, hence to be fully alive, that I draw what the Chinese call 'The Ten Thousand Things' around me. Drawing is the discipline by which I constantly rediscover the world. I have learned that what I have not drawn, I have never really seen, and that when I start drawing an ordinary thing, I realise how extraordinary it is, sheer miracle. (Franck 1973)

After this teaching, the children drew the same subjects again.

The scraps of paper exercise is important for me (Figure 1.4). Later, I was to come across a variant of it by Andrea Durrant called Consequences. Following her suggestion, towards the end of the project I gave all the children more scraps of paper and asked each one to draw a line across it. They then had to pass their paper on to the next person, and everybody had to draw a line that was different to the first line (Figure 1.5) and so on. Another variant uses pieces of paper divided into rectangles (Figure 1.6). It is important to note that in the first version of this exercise, children are relatively free, even uncontrolled, in the marks they make. In the second, there is a useful interaction between different people's lines. In the third version, when the paper is divided into rectangles, they have to be more controlled in their marks, so that their pencils don't go over the lines.

Andrea Durrant scribbled on an early draft of this book: 'not scraps of paper – small pieces of quality paper … scrap implies cheap, slapdash!' I take her point. Children should have the best in terms of material and teaching available to them. All too often they are offered the cheap – in terms of food, for example. But an artist or a writer sitting on a bus who is suddenly struck with an idea about how to move a project forward that has been stuck or blocked for a length of time does not wait to get back to her quality materials. She scribbles down notes on whatever scraps of paper are available: the back of an envelope, the margin of the daily paper, the bus ticket.

When I asked the children to draw the faces again, I asked them to write on their paper as they saw fit notes about what they were looking at, using the word 'like' as much as possible in order to introduce similes. I don't know why children have been trained in classrooms to separate writing from drawing. It may well be that the traditional curriculum grid has imposed this distinction. It is certainly a false one, and, although current legislation reinforces it, it should be broken down. When children draw they are not only learning about art, they are learning about the effective use of their language to describe the world around them – in this case, their friends' faces. This learning might be in conversation. But it might also be unexpressed; it might simply be in thought. Words surface as they draw, as I have suggested in my poem at the beginning of this book. This learning will give them power. It will help them to see that their perception of the world is valid. It will give them strength. It will help them to stand up for themselves.

Let's now turn to the second drawings by Anna, Rosemary and Lindsay. I also include a drawing by Jonathan. Anna's drawing has taken on life (Figure 1.7). She hardly saw her model's hair, to judge from her first picture, let alone imagined it. But now, after focused observation, Anna has drawn that hair with waves and various tones ('like a piece of silk', as she writes). Like real hair, it is represented differently on different parts of the head. The eyes, farther apart and lower down the face (though not low enough for the sake of photographic correctness) look in two directions at once, like the eyes of many of Picasso's women seen over a period of time looking in different directions. The lips (Anna has written) are 'like an exotic flower'. Only by drawing, I suggest, would the writer have invented this simile, which is better than most of the similes for lips that I have heard in popular song ('like cherries … sweet as wine … rubies').

1.4

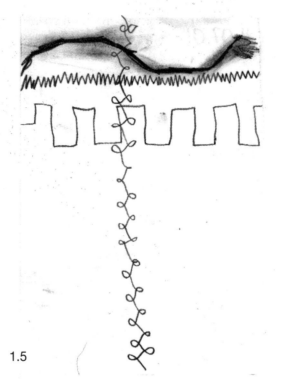

1.5

1.6

I am glad to say that Rosemary (Figure 1.8) and Jonathan (Figure 1.9) have taken the instruction to use different kinds of pencil mark (rule 3) literally. I am sorry to say that this never happened again. They have reproduced the wriggly lines that they had innocently scribbled on their scrap of paper, not knowing, of course, that I would ask them to use them in a serious drawing, for the form of the face, the details of it, even the texture of it. Neither of them was pleased with the result ('I like my first drawing best', said Rosemary). Even Pam, the teacher, was unsure. 'I don't think Fred meant quite that' she said to one of them, as she walked around the room, looking at the drawings as they progressed.

But to me the second set of drawings has a vigour the first set lacks, and I felt they were beautiful examples of both teaching and art opening out into new possibilities. It is important to try to see what children do that is detached from the teaching – that sometimes even subverts it. They learn, not only because of what we teach, but in spite of it. Among the similes these two children came up with were: 'eyes like mud … ears like a maze … nose like a slide … lips like pink leaves … teeth like yellow stars'.

Lindsay's drawing (Figure 1.10) is the least different from the first one, but because it is bigger, it has a new strength, and a hint of character comes across in the expression.

I was encouraged by this session, which lasted about half an hour. The main thrust of my argument – about teaching drawing, its importance, and a method – is contained in this section and underlies everything I write from now on. To sum up the method given above (the four rules) it is concerned with the children trusting themselves, their vision and their lines.

The cats

In my choice of subjects in all these lessons, I have been guided by the belief that any kind of stimulation that helps children to understand better those objects and creatures that they see around them will contribute to their intellectual growth. Faces, with all their differences in terms of colour, shape, texture and so on, seem worth understanding. So do cats: their tidy pose when sitting, tails tucked round their fronts; their evident concentration on a task; their independence; and their purring.

Not teaching the cats

After break, I did the same lesson with the older juniors, with one difference: the subject of their drawings was not present in the room, it was merely present in their imaginations. I use the word 'merely' in an ironic sense – the presence of a subject in a focused mind is often even more close to an artist than a subject present in the same room. I was once asked: 'how can you draw yourself gardening, or loading the washing machine?' That question hangs limply, like a Daliesque clock, from a notion that drawing is a representation of 'reality' (a word that, as Nabokov said, means

Her hair is like a pice of silk.

Her lips are like an exzotiz glower.

Her nose reminds me of a mountain

Her frexeles remuned me of pebbles on the sand.

Her eye lashes are like thin bits of cole.

Her eye brows are lake black as

Her eye balls, are like blueberrys.

Her ears are like

picture of Georgia O

1.7

her lips are like pink leaves
her ears are like a Maze,
her neck is like a swan

her eye lashes are like tadpoles

her eyebrows are like long grass

Kate

her hair is like shiny wood
her eyes are like balls of blue
her nose is like a slide

1.8

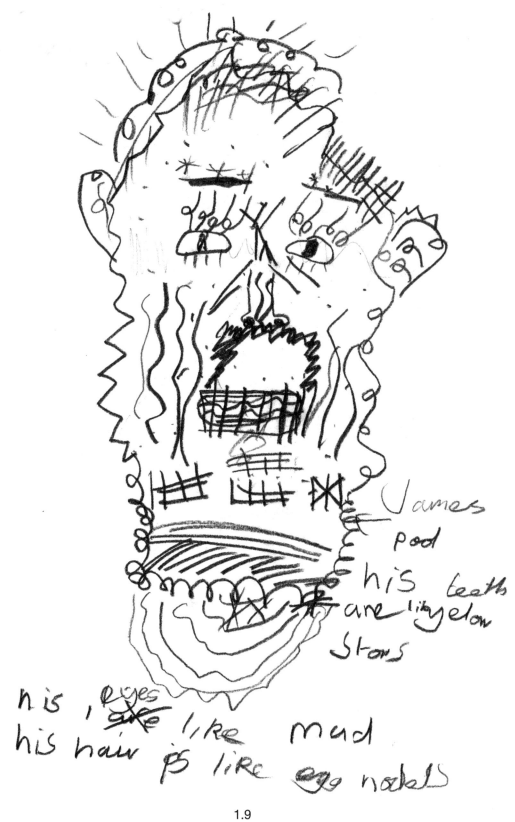

James
pod
his teeth
are like yelow
Stons

his , eyes
his hair like mud
is like egg nodels

1.9

her lips are like red dark apples
her hair is like brown curly   sea weed
her nose is like a worm hana

1.10

nothing without its quotation marks: your reality? my reality? yours or mine with our imagination engaged, or with our imagination left to one side?). Drawing does try to represent a natural 'reality', of course. That is its first function. But it also tries to represent a 'reality' that lives mostly in the imagination. It may look as though Leonardo is merely recording: but he is also using his imagination, and an electrical relationship between his recording and his imagination. I can imagine myself gardening and loading the washing machine; and I can draw what I imagine.

I told the children to draw a cat – nothing more. Here are drawings by Henry, Emily, Olivia and Sophie (Figures 1.11 to 1.14). These drawings are even more conventional than the first face drawings. Sophie has made two attempts; both are cartoon figures with no discernible meaning and with no vigour. Olivia's sleeping cat has a little more life, but it is over-tentative in technique. Henry and Emily make pleasant little images.

Teaching the cats

I then taught the children the lesson that I have already described. I also told them they could only see the cat (in Hamlet's words) 'in [their] minds' eye[s]'. They closed their 'outside eyes' and covered them with their hands. 'Art', says Leonardo, 'has to be put in prison before it can be set free'. Children can be profitably imprisoned inside their heads, deprived briefly of the sense of sight, and the result will be heightened drawing. It was important that the subject was not just any cat but 'your cat, the cat from down the road, your grandma's cat, that stray who comes into your garden and annoys your parents'.

I told the children that they should picture the cat doing something, not just 'standing there or sitting about or lying on the carpet', and I told a story to help them, in the present tense, based on watching my own cat: 'The cat has just woken up. It stretches – front legs first, then back legs. Then its middle. Yawns. Suddenly it is outside – in the garden, in the street, running. Look at its legs with your mind's eye. Note how they move. Now the cat is stalking something. Look at its eyes as it does so …' The rest of the story (which the children listened to in the empowering dark silence of that prison cell, that silence that freed their imaginations) concerned the cat eating, drinking and sleeping, or pricking its ears back in alertness to some possible danger. I told the story entirely in the present tense because that has a more immediate impact than the past. It is happening now, and I want the drawings to look as though they are happening now.

In all this preparation, I was helping the children to bring their imagination into play. To draw well is not just to look at what is immediately observable, but to imagine it. Drawing means making the observable ours.

Look at the second set of drawings by Olivia, Alex, Henry, Emily and Sophie (Figures 1.15 to 1.19). I think the differences here are even more striking than they were with the faces the younger children drew. Olivia's drawing (Figure 1.15) has lost all its tentativeness. We can see balance in the hind legs and vigour in the tail. How well observed (with her mind's eye, remember – her imagination) the expression on the face is. She has used techniques she hadn't thought of before. She

1.11

1.12

1.13

1.14

didn't need to be taught that smudging the base of her drawing would be effective: she has discovered it for herself. She writes on her drawing, after some excellent similes, 'the cat is my cat'. We knew that already. She makes her ownership of the cat (and her sense of that ownership) more certain with her drawing.

The cat cliché of Alex's first drawing (not given here) takes on a new life (Figure 1.16). Henry produces some excellent similes (Figure 1.17): 'The cat's eyes are like a goalkeeper staring at you when you take a penalty … the cat's paws remind me of wildebeests' footprints.' Perhaps Henry (who is, not irrelevantly, an accomplished goalkeeper) sees himself (or has been seen by others) as a less effective artist than some of the other children. The legs of his cat are carpentered onto the body, as though with a mortise and tenon joint, rather than an organic part of it. Similarly, the fur has been Velcro'd onto its back. The figure looks like an aeroplane's fuselage on legs. As I type this first draft, I wonder how his work will develop. But I can sense his imagination working in his writing. Emily's cat has moved from cuteness to character ('the claws are sharp, quick and lethal') (Figure 1.18) while Sophie's new page (Figure 1.19) is stiff with learning. The drawing of the cat's face captures a relaxing cat perfectly, and the instruction about ways of using a pencil (which is central to all the work illustrated in this book) has led her to incorporate great vigour in the body of the cat and, in particular, its tail. And look at her writing: 'I like the way that her fur is always shiny, and her long silky whiskers remind me of the grass covered in dew … She is a very lazy cat. She loves to be brushed and she belongs to my Grandma.'

It was important to ask the children to write notes on their drawings because the writing showed what was going on in the children's heads. It gives us a glimpse of the imagination at work. Also, it taught them a lesson about the nature of learning: it is a mixed business. We learn, adult and child alike, both through words and through visual images. Being set free to draw *and* write (rather than just one or the other), is intensively educational because it involves choice. I had learned the lesson of allowing children to mix drawing and writing in the mid-eighties when an art educationalist called Maurice Rubens came to the school where I was then head teacher. This is my memory of that occasion, tidied up, as it no doubt is, by the passing of time. He told me that there was some 'fine writing' in the school. He waited for this to sink in, and then he said, 'There is some fine drawing too.' Pause. Then: 'Why do you always separate the two?' Ever since, whenever I have had the opportunity, I have encouraged children to draw and write when learning about objects in a close observational way. Often, when they are making graphic lines on their paper, thinking about their drawing strengthens their verbal grasp on the images they are drawing. It is impossible to prove this, of course, but I am convinced that all lines are what Paul Klee calls 'lines into knowledge'. All lines deal, one way or another, with the imagination.

Mixing drawing and writing taught us, the teachers, a lesson, too. Consider how much less evidence of learning there would have been in Sophie's picture had she not written on it. We are more able to assess children's understanding if we allow them to use words during activities when, traditionally, words have not been encouraged. (This is a drawing lesson. This is a science lesson.) Think again about Leonardo and the variety of marks he chose to make in order to understand. He almost certainly did not 'finish' his writing before 'doing' his drawing, or the other

The cats eyes are like
playfull childs,

The cats movement is like a
sudden leap,

Its fur, like rough velvet
in many places,

.The cats name, 'Charlie'cat'
is the name I know,

The cat is my cat

1.15

I like her
fir it has many
different patter

this cats name is tinker
I like the way she runs.
I like her tail its nice and soft.
I like her eyes you can see them in
the dark.

1.16

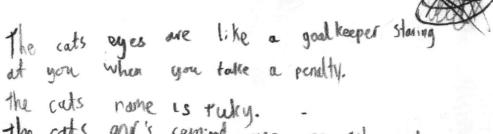

The cats eyes are like a goalkeeper staring at you when you take a penalty.

the cats name is ruky.

The cats ear's remind me of silver shining spikes.

The cats paws remind me of wilderbeast's foot frints.

The cats fur feels like rough grass.

the cats tails is like swinging a rope around.

1.17

The cats eyes remind me of a deep shining emerald sparkling.
The cats paws remind me of soft whispy white clouds on a Summers day
The cats face is like the golden rays of sunshine when he purrs with
delight. luxury
The cats fur feels like ! feather pillows
The cats claws are sharp quick and lethal.

Emily H age 10
5.4.10
B

1.18

1.19

This cats name is Lulu
Her eyes remind me of Saphrons glittering
in the sun,
I like the way that her fur is
always shiny and her long
silky whiskers remind me of
the grass covered in dew.

She is a dead.
black and it reminds
me of the black
sky. She is a very
lazy cat. She loves to be brushed and she belongs
to my Grandma. to be brushed and she belongs

way around. I thought of this when a teacher asked me when a group of six-year-olds should be 'allowed' to stop writing and draw. The children should draw and write as the spirit of learning takes them, because each activity feeds the other.

Drawing and writing feed other areas of educational experience too. For example, I asked children in another school (who had also drawn and written about cats as I have described above), to dance like cats. At first, they became what I call cartoon cats: they dropped to all fours and moved around the room mewing. It looked like a hall full of Toms from Tom and Jerry. It was embarrassing. They were stereotypes. I told them they didn't have to *look* like cats in general – they had to *behave* like a *particular* cat. I asked them to think again about that cat. We discussed aspects of cat behaviour: that strange concentration that I mentioned before, the lightness of the touch of their feet on the ground, the startled turn of the neck and head, the apparent keenness to be methodical when washing. I read them poetry about cats: Christopher Smart's 'For I will consider my cat Jeoffry' (from *Jubilate Agno* and collected in Sedgwick 2000) and George Macbeth's 'Fourteen Ways of Touching the Peter' (in Mackay 1969).

The children danced, and this time they were not cartoons. They had imagined themselves closer to what a cat's behaviour is like. They had forgotten the need to be on all fours. Their eyes mimed cat-like concentration, and sometimes they rested with that immaculate tidiness a cat has when content: when it is alert, clean and fed.

They also wrote about cats:

It moves slowly and softly
a little bit at a time.

It moves cautiously towards the door,
back arching, legs moving,
then enjoying every moment of its milk.

Cat with an angry look
with back arching like a
rainbow without colours.

It has marble eyes
and a velvet nose foam mouth
and torn ears.

The essential difference between asking children to draw from a model present in the classroom – the face, for example – and to draw from a model present in 'the mind's eye', like the cat, is this. In the latter case, the imagination is more strongly called on. It has to work at top pressure. That is not to say that the imagination is not required in conventional observational drawing. A good drawing is far more than a record of features; it helps the artist to see inside a character, to see what Gerard Manley Hopkins called the 'inscape' of a person.

I drove back through the dubious spring morning, wondering what other subjects I could ask the children to draw, what other graphic tools they might use apart from pencils, and how I might help them develop their techniques. In this chapter, I have reproduced almost all the drawings the children made. From now on, considerations of how much learning I can find in individual drawings will dictate which drawings I use.

2 African Carvings and an Ancient Greek Horse

Over the Easter holidays, I spent hours looking at about 60 drawings of faces and cats that I had brought away from Bealings. I was worried about which of the children I was going to ask to make up the group whose work (alongside the work of three Key Stage 1 children who had not taken part in the first session) would form the database of this book. I show here four cats drawn by children whose work was not otherwise included to demonstrate the power of what the children did that day. They suggest, I hope, that I did not choose only work from those who teachers and children themselves often call 'the best artists': here is the work of four of them that I excluded (Figures 2.1 to 2.4).

Looking at them now, I note again how vivid the children's notes are. The cats are:

> sleek as a snake … can strike like a sword … eyes are as good as a magnifying glass … eyes are like searchlights … the tail is like a whip … the tongue feels like a cactus … the pads resemble cushions … when she runs she hobbles like an old person with her walking stick … the place where her missing leg was is like a tree stump …

In these notes, it is easy to see that the work on similes described in Chapter 1 worked. It would not have worked so well had the children not drawn the cats featured in their imaginations.

All the drawings had strengths, both in visual and written lines. I was especially interested in drawings that showed evidence of the children taking my four rules of drawing seriously. Rosemary and Jonathan, therefore, were in the group from the start. Both these drawings show that the two children had decided to obey me (what teacher can resist obedience?) in spite of how absurd my demands were. And both drawings say, implicitly, to hell with photographic verisimilitude.

A criterion such as 'the best artists' would probably have less to teach me if only because they had learned so much already. And what is the point of a book about enabling children's learning through drawing if it only discusses the work of children perceived as the best? The least able would have more to show if they took on board what I was trying to teach, because I would be able to see more progress. My choice of which children to use was also about democracy. Much as we are, as teachers, entranced by what the evidently clever children can do, we must be

Her ears
are like brown
leaves in the
Autumn

when she
runs she
hobbles like
an old person
with walking
stick

Her ~~this~~ name is
Florence or
Tripod.

The place
where her missing
leg was is
like a tree stump.

Her tail is like a
branch bending in
the wind.
Its ~~eyes~~ ~~are~~ remind
Me of head leaves en
red

2.1

The cats eyes are like bombs in the midnight sky

The cats tonge like a cactus

The cats pad Resemble cussions

The cats tail'e feels like a

The cats name is winsen

2.2

The eyes are like Srearch lights.
The ears are like a radar.
The tail is like a whip.
The cats name is Reece.
The fur is like Velcro.

The cat likes moise.
The cat likes Hunting.
The cat Is mine.

2.3

He can smell like

His eyes are as good as a magnifying glass

He's as ginger as gingerbread

His ears are like teeth

His eyes are like head lamps

This cat is running

He is as sleek as a snake

He can strike like a sword

Age 8
Year. 4

2.4

attracted by what we dismissively (and unprofessionally) call the others – 'the less able', 'the non-creative' – who struggle with what the National Curriculum and we as individual teachers challenge them with.

Also, I was worried about offending children whom I knew well. I was almost sure that they would see this exercise as picking the best artists: it was for them, a kind of competition. How could it not be, given the increasingly competitive nature of the school system in recent years? The school league tables; the levels that the children have had to clamber onto; those horrible graphs in some schools (though, emphatically, not Bealings) showing which children had got the most stars. To detach what I was doing from all that was easy for me, as it was for Duncan and his staff. I doubt whether it was as easy for the children. Nevertheless, I suspect any disappointment wore off quickly, children being resilient and realistic.

'My four rules of drawing.' How arrogant that sounds! I write as though I had worked out how children should draw. This is ridiculous, as you know, because you have other rules for drawing and you too will guarantee that your rules will improve the drawing in a school overnight (I would like to hear about them). Andrea Durrant has her rules. But I leave my first paragraph there, as an example of what teachers have often said, often implied: they know. And I leave it there as a warning to me for the rest of the book. Will I be alert enough to see what children learn through and about their drawing that goes beyond, or even subverts, my four rules? I hope I will change my mind about my rules, because, as the harper sings in Blake's *A Marriage of Heaven and Hell*, 'The man that never alters his opinion is like standing water, and breeds reptiles of the mind.'

In the end, I chose a mixture of children. I tried to understand the drawings, and what learning was going on in the triangle that I mentally visualise when I watch children draw. The three points of that triangle are the child's eye, the child's hand, and the subject of the drawing. For me, this triangle is an emblem, a symbol of what education is. I imagine the sides of it singing and zipping with electric changes as the child talks, draws, reflects, writes and learns. The charges move unpredictably at various speeds in both directions as the child works: he brings to what he is learning what he already knows. This is in vivid contrast to the official model for education, which is a speaking tube down which the teacher speaks, or a catching cradle into which the teacher hurls knowledge. The child's banal task, in this model, is to hear and record, or catch, what he can, with as little discomfort as he can manage.

I drafted and redrafted the first chapter, correcting the usual problems of style (the ones that I spotted, anyway) and tried to make sure that I was saying something approximating as close as possible to what I wanted to say. T. S. Eliot's phrase about 'the interminable struggle between words and meanings' came to mind as I looked over what I had written, as it always does. In all this tiresome activity, I was learning. And, as I have insisted, if I do not learn as I teach, and if I do not reflect on my teaching, I am not teaching. If I do not learn as I write, I am writing in a limited way.

I sent a copy of the chapter to Duncan for his comments. He approved of nearly all of it, but said that his children were less privileged than I had originally written. I asked him to write a note about aspects of the school of which I was ignorant, and he said he would. But he was moving house, and had much at the front of his mind.

It is worth mentioning this, because much writing about teaching seems to suggest that teachers live in a world without normal concerns, such as marriage, birth, estrangement, divorce, moving house, worrying about children at university, and the rest.

After the holidays, I went back to Bealings. What was I to offer the children next? I had gone through options in my head, and, typically, didn't rest on one until five minutes before I left the house. I thought guiltily about all those preparation notes I used to make on teaching practice (Aims of the lesson ... Visual aids ... Method ... Question and Answer ... Lesson evaluation). I thought less guiltily, but with sympathy, about the useless scribbling tasks about short-, medium-, and long-term plans that have been imposed on young teachers now.

In our house we have a number of inexpensive objects from different cultures – mostly African – bought at various times from shops run by collectors who have lived in Nigeria, Mali and Malawi. The darkness, and that quality of being rooted in the earth (so different from the more ethereal quality of much European art, which so often seems to be aiming at the sky) appeals to us.

We have Yoruba twins from Nigeria, carved to celebrate the birth of real twins. This event (and carving to celebrate it) happens frequently in that culture and that country. These two figures are clothed in rough hessian-like material, and decorated with sea shells. They have sombre faces. They normally live high on a wall in our dining room, on little shelves made for the purpose. We have a pair of Benin bronzes: a king and a queen, wearing crowns and jewellery (they mostly stay in my wife's workroom). We have a young woman with handsome features, a reflective expression and an intricate hairstyle, including plaits. She stays in my study, the source of some comfort when the word processor is hard to motivate. We have a kneeling woman with a pot on her head. She is peripatetic, but stays mostly under a lamp in the living room. And, very different from the African figures, we have a replica of a first-century BC Greek horse, bought on the island of Samos on our most recent holiday together and usually to be found on the mantelpiece under the twins. This horse is evidently a toy, having wheels.

All these objects stand for an aim of mine in all my teaching: to build a bridge between art and drawing on the one hand, and on the other creating an atmosphere of respect for all humanity. It is hard not to write in clichés about this. Multiculturalism has become worse than a cliché: it has become a platitude. I want to suggest, however, that educationally the idea of respect for our fellow human beings is embedded in our idea of what art is: what it means to those who create it, and what it teaches us about those who create it. That is why the notion of a racist artist is either meaningless or obscene. Art insists on the humanity of other human beings. Take out the person, and you take out art, as the poet John Cotton wrote. That does not mean that art that doesn't represent humans is not true art (Islamic art, modern abstract paintings, still lives, paintings of animals) but it does mean art is not art unless it is part of humanity's attempt to understand itself.

The horse, like the drawings in the Pileta caves – and like, to take more familiar examples from life in the UK today, ancient churches and cathedrals – raises the question of respect for human beings in the past. The ideas those people entertained can seem as strange to us now as the ideas of people from different cultures living in the same times as ourselves. I want to consider briefly the idea that, much as children have to learn to respect people of different cultures from their own, they also have to learn to respect people of the past, and their cultures. Also, the future, and respect for human beings in the future, leads to work on the environment that is beyond the scope of this book.

I packed all these items in a plastic crate and set off. I drove through showers and bright April light. Once more, I asked the children to do the experiment with different pencil marks. The three children from Key Stage 1 – Alistair, Jeremy and William – were with us for the first time, and the older children explained to them what was required. I then introduced the children to the objects, one by one, and asked them to choose the piece that they would most like to draw.

The children rejected two of the objects: the pot-carrier and the female twin. I suspect that the reason for the rejection was the exposed female breasts. One of the older girls, Alex, seemed embarrassed by them, and this embarrassment spread to the other children. Duncan told me later that I might have chosen other children who wouldn't have shown any embarrassment at all.

Figures 2.5 to 2.8 show drawings of the female head; Figures 2.9 to 2.11 show drawings of the Benin bronzes; and Figures 2.12 to 2.14 show drawings of the Greek horse (note the drawings have been reduced in size).

We worked in the little school hall. Six of the children sat at a round table, four around a rectangular one, and the last two were happy to work laying on their fronts on the floor with the subjects of their drawings raised on the piano stool in front of them. As they started work, I looked hard at their progress, seeking evidence of learning styles and for evidence of what had been learnt in the first session. Because I have always thrived on the encouragement of my seniors (and my editors, come to that) and wilted under their discouragement (ditto), I praised everything the children did that morning that seemed to be a sincere attempt to work to the four rules. I also praised some things they did that went beyond the rules that provided evidence of thought and innate talent.

Every child had produced something strong. But Henry, who had drawn the least effectively in the first session, was tentative, rejecting this time any definite dark lines. He took over half an hour longer than anyone else in the group, and spent the first ten minutes drawing the feet of the male twin. He took enormous care, and kept looking. But while his drawings in the first lesson were built up with strong dark lines, his new drawing was too faint to reproduce here. I felt that he was too anxious to get the proportions right, and less concerned with capturing the feeling of the male twin from Nigeria. Later, Henry wrote: 'When I draw I think of the perfect picture. I prefer colour because it makes it bright. When I finish I think does it look the same [as the subject], have I done enough detail?' Henry had that common conviction that photographic accuracy was all-important in drawing; that feeling matters had probably never occurred to him. Or worse, no one had ever taught him that feeling matters – a common problem with children in an age when they are surrounded with images in photography, film, prints, paintings and drawing that value above all photographic correctness. This is, in fact, an age when that need for that correctness is largely unquestioned except among an artistic intelligentsia remote from most children.

I like it because it has hair and a smooth face

It reminds me of a person from Holland and it looks like she's been burnt on one side of the face

2.5

Like the way her hair looks like spaggity
He hair feels like the bark on a tree
I think she thinking about her family and
the people she loves. She also looks
sad and upset she looks as though
shes from a hot country.

2.6

I like the way that the hair
feels like shells. I like the way
her ~~hair~~ ~~plates~~ plaits feel like long
twigs. I like the
her neck is very
Smooth.

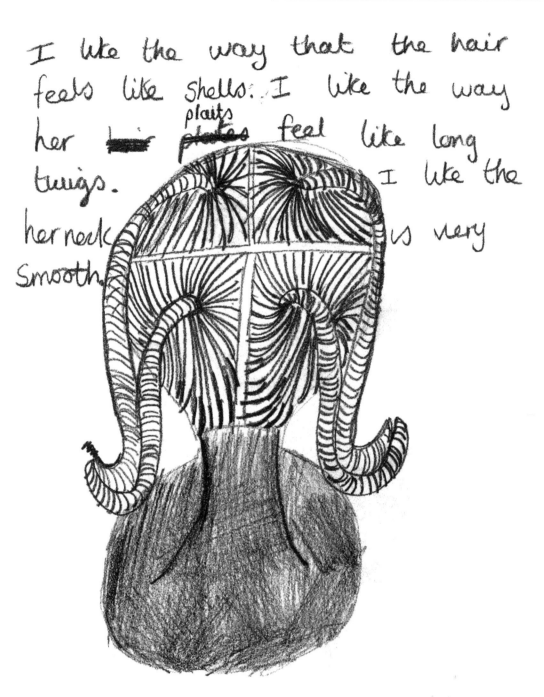

2.7

I like the hair it is bumpy like Mountain
and hills and valleys. I like the soft
brown Couler   that reminds me of
dry   Soil.
the   Smooth
neck   reminds
me   of
Shiny   piano
keys.   the
Scratche   and
scrapes   remind
me of   little
rivers   and
Seas.

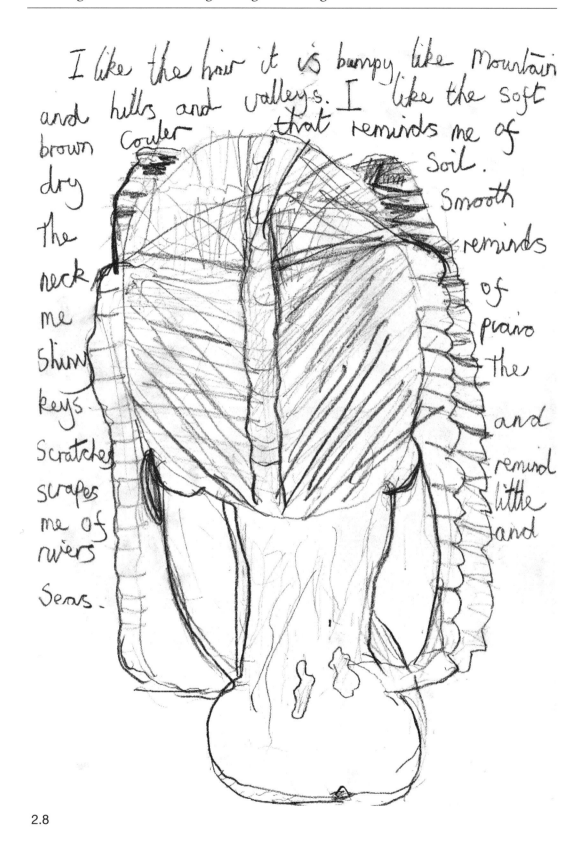

2.8

But I was encouraged to see that Henry, alone among the children, varied his style from lesson to lesson. Rosemary's drawing (Figure 2.5) has the interesting note 'it looks like she's been burnt on one side of the face' (Figure 2.6). Sophie and Emily (Figure 2.8) worked as they had before, with great confidence in their lines, crashing in after quick thought. Sophie in particular used the many ways of making marks that I had helped the children demonstrate to themselves with great verve. I doubt whether she would have achieved the contrast between the main drawing lines and the shading on the face without that lesson. Sophie wrote on her paper: 'Her hair feels like the bark on a tree ... She is thinking about her family and the people she loves ...' Emily filled her page. Her work always looks to me as though learning is bursting the boundaries of the paper she has been given, and I think this is a suitable metaphor for children. They are always potentially bursting the boundaries of what the official schooling system gives them. She wrote beautifully. My contention is that the act of purposeful drawing has led directly to this writing: 'the soft brown colour ... reminds me of dry soil. The smooth neck reminds me of shiny piano keys ...'

Alex was confident, too, her drawing exact and almost geometric (Figure 2.7). The plaits look like worms crawling out of an apple; an effect, I am sure, not intended. How different her drawing is from Emily's. How much they are subconsciously, or unconsciously, saying about themselves. Arguably, there is nothing that tells the people around us as much about our inner lives than our learning styles. When I looked more closely at the work of the children working on the female head, I was struck again at the sharpness of the observation shown in the notes that the children had written on their paper. Anna had got the proportions wrong from the start (her drawing is not reproduced here) in contrast to Sophie, who has got things conventionally right. But Anna has written: 'Her plaits look like little waves from the sea. Her neck looks like scales from a chameleon.' So the attention Anna has paid to the head has paid dividends in her writing.

I watched Olivia's drawing of the horse grow (Figure 2.12: I note now that her age is 'nearly 10'). She was sitting at the front end of it and I knew that this would present her with an unfamiliar challenge. I had been struck with her second drawing of the cat rearing up and wondered how she would cope with this drawing. Already a very personal style is emerging in her work. She readily draws sketching lines on her paper, then emphasising the line she eventually sees as the right one. She seems very ready to see lines as provisional.

Olivia was sitting with Alistair (Figure 2.13) and William (Figure 2.14), both six years old and new to the group. William's drawing is almost a symbol of the horse rather than an analytical representation of it. I resolved that the next time I met the group I would work individually with William on looking. Alistair, on the other hand, has made a drawing surprisingly mature and analytical. I felt that he would benefit from a longer experience at the many kinds of lines rule.

She is very
cold and
heveay and
She look like
a lady from
a hot place.
A she could
be a
Pupet.

2.9

She looks like a lady
Who lives in a hot
place that was
looking for
water

Shes cold
and very
light
and its
metal
with a
hole at
the bottom

She s
quite
rusty and
it looks
like shes
about 80
years old

2.10

I think if looks like if is real

2.11

Lindsay is another child whose personal style is evident. She makes dark smudgy messes from the beginning (Figure 2.10), and her drawings have great presence. She shows an attack on her drawing of the queen that many adult artists would envy. 'The lady … lives in a hot place … looking for water …' She was working with Jeremy, another Key Stage 1 newcomer (Figure 2.9). None of the children had used the more extreme scribbles this time, as Rosemary and Jonathan had in the first session. I regretted this as these marks often give drawings an oddity that I find interesting. While that lesson undoubtedly enriched nearly all the drawings done subsequently, the eccentric quality of Rosemary's and Jonathan's drawings (pp. 19 and 20) in the first session never re-emerged.

It feels rough and cold.
The horse looks Dark
and old,
It moves stedily and
slowly on its wheels

2.12

It feels like Solid wood

It was ment to pull
coal

2.13

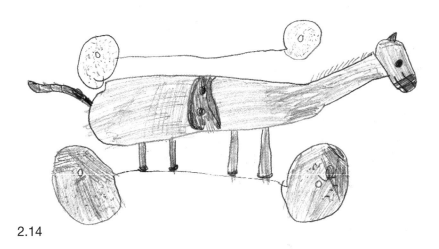

2.14

Two boys produced drawings of the Benin bronzes that impressed me. Both Jonathan's and Jeremy's drawings (FIgures 2.9 and 2.11) have eyes that are full of feeling, and the pencil marks, varied in terms of weight and direction, again support my contention that teaching about what a pencil can do contributes more to art teaching than most teachers realise. It made for a kind of discovery. Jonathan is right when he writes on his paper, 'I think it looks like it is real.'

I wrote notes at this point: 'I will put the children on individual programmes ... William and Alistair need lots more work in different kinds of marks ... Next time, it will be time to move the more experienced children on to different graphic tools, perhaps, while giving the younger children further practice in using pencils ...'

Figures 2.15 and 2.16 show the children drawing, respectively, the female head and the Greek horse. Also on the tables are the scraps of paper used to discover different ways of making marks (both figures), and one of the Benin bronzes (Figure 2.16).

2.15

2.16

3 Biros

This chapter is about children working with ballpoint pens. But I need first to discuss a certain kind of school.

Habitat and hessian schools

Head teachers of Habitat and hessian schools have long despised certain graphic instruments, and zealously guarded their children from them. They deem felt tip pens, for example, and, relevant to this chapter, ballpoint pens, as 'inappropriate' for children and art. 'Inappropriate' is a cant word used in the education system by those who disapprove of something, but who don't want to, or (more likely) can't be bothered to, argue their case. These head teachers only accept traditional mark-makers in their schools: pencil, of course, charcoal, and pen and ink – mark-makers that can be associated easily with traditional drawings.

Some years ago, while working with a group of infants who were drawing parts of their Victorian school building, I asked the head teacher if the school had any other graphic tools that the children could use apart from the pencils with which the children had already made drawings. 'Like what?' he asked. 'Well, felt tips …?' I said. He put his hands up, palms forward in front of his shoulders, and sent for the garlic. 'I don't have felt tips in my school', he said, like a priest asked if he kept equipment for a black mass in his vestry. Perhaps coincidentally, I have never been asked back to this school.

Before I get closer to the ballpoints, and how useful they are, I had better explain the epithets 'Habitat' and 'hessian', and what I mean by them. I have worked, for over 30 years, with head teachers one of whose evident aims is to transform their schools into little art galleries. I do not mean by this that their aim is to make institutions that, among other things, encourage and display innovative visual art. Definitely not. These head teachers hope that their teachers will arrange 'pleasing' displays of children's drawings, writing, pottery and the like. These displays are often decorated with 'drapes', pieces of fabric of tasteful hue – beige, fawn, earth brown, green – and pattern, usually influenced by William Morris, hanging behind or beside the objects. Sometimes these drapes are 'ruched' (ruche: 'a pleated or gathered strip of fabric used for trimming'). There are still schools where the ruching skill is prized above the ability to teach children to read or walk safely across the road. I met a young teacher, Hannah Sharples, who had done her PGCE year at a college where the pleats in drapes for display had to be exactly 'two centimetres wide'. It was what you might call the training wing of the hessian movement. She wrote a poem, alongside her children:

> I used to measure my two centimetre pleats
> But now I teach in the real world.

The term 'Habitat' struck me as appropriate for the appearance of these schools about 20 years ago, and has stayed with me ever since. Walk around buildings like this – through the security system, into the entrance hall, down corridors, into classrooms, through halls and gyms, back (especially, if you can get in here) to the head teacher's study – and you will find little wooden boxes covered with a carpet-like material, nearly always in a shade of brown, or fawn, or beige. I have often been reminded of the early Habitat stores, with their unremitting good taste: plain colours, simple shapes and clean spaces.

These displays are most evident, significantly, in entrance halls. They are, at least in part, window dressing, and they tell you (whatever they are meant to tell you) that someone has spent time away from learning, from education. They have spent time arranging jars of teazles, pots, little circles of sea shells, skulls of animals, or parts of a car engine.

The difference between these displays and those at Kettle's Yard is that the former are just that: displays. The latter are, essentially, not displays at all, but part of a working house. You are free to pick up books from the shelves, sit in a chair, and read. You can touch the carvings. You do actually trip over corners of rugs. The house is interactive. In contrast, the school displays carry an unwritten notice saying DO NOT TOUCH. In many schools, especially those in working-class communities, they serve as statements of middle-class superiority.

It is all there, in that entrance hall display. The tasteful background in one or more of the prescribed colours; the drapes at the side in matching colours. This is a display about transport, so there are cartwheels, bike wheels and steering wheels; old postcards of buses and cars and penny-farthings; books; a few rail tickets; children's drawings and paintings. And there are the labels. Fifteen years ago they would have been in neat italics – now they are in a computer typeface. It strikes you, as you wait, that no one else is looking at this wall. Children, teachers, learning support assistants, secretaries and parents all hurry by without giving it a first, let alone a second, glance. Life is being lived.

Peter Dixon, the poet and art teacher/lecturer/writer, has a marvellous page about mounting, hessian and drapes in one of the funny, truthful books (mostly undated) he wrote, typed, illustrated and published himself. It shows a child's picture at various stages. At the first stage, it is on the wall, unmounted (this means: 'I respect your work and I have pinned it up carefully'). At the second stage, the picture is double-mounted ('I respect your work ever such a lot and I've double-mounted it on black sugar paper'). At the third and fourth stages, it has further mounts. (Third: 'I respect your work amazingly so I've triple-mounted it on black with a purple piece as well …' The fourth stage: 'You will never believe how much I appreciate your work. It is beyond comprehension. It is on black, purple and yellow!') At the fifth stage, the picture is quadruple-mounted, and stuck onto the background with 'plastitak because I don't want pins tearing the hessian'. Finally, the picture is displayed with a drape. ('I respect your work to such an incredibly unbelievable extent that I am going to swathe it with my old curtains …')

Dixon makes an important point here. Teachers often spend more money, more time and more effort in the display of a child's work than they spend, or allow the child to spend, in the making of it. A piece of A4 paper and an HB pencil will do for the original drawing, but, for whatever reason, the display requires sugar paper and other kinds of paper, hessian, ruched drapes and space. I made these points once at a conference for teachers. As we filed out for coffee, I overheard a young teacher say, 'Well, I like my children's work to be put up nicely.' Of course, children's work – or in this case their drawings – should be displayed respectfully. This teacher had a point.

But there are many ways of displaying art that do not involve enormous investment in time, money and effort, thus freeing that time, money and effort for teaching and learning. First, every lesson should end with an exhibition when each piece is put down on a table, or on the floor, and all the children, teachers, learning assistants, visitors and even (should she be available) the head teacher should look at them. This is the time for critical comment; comment that will be far more relevant, in part because it is immediate, in part because it is made to the artists, than any comment made in front of a formal display.

Second, work could be pinned to the wall by the children at the end of the lesson. Deciding how to display their work is part of their art education, a point always missed by followers of the Habitat and hessian movement, who assume that once a drawing is finished, the child loses possession of it and any decision as to its future passes to the teacher. Third, there should be a formal exhibition of children's work, when parents, the head teacher or other guests are invited to view it. Then the mounting etc. becomes important (though not, in my view, the ruched drapes).

Head teachers of Habitat and hessian schools have other obsessions. In fact, they have phobias. They do not allow children to use screwed-up tissue paper or wax crayons. I know this because I was a head teacher influenced by Habitat and hessian. I would not allow templates in my school. Obviously, I think this ban more justified: templates in art restrict children's drawing to the teacher's designs. I recall a circular display on the subject of the zodiac where the proportions of the whole design – and of each little image within it – were chosen and drawn by the teacher. The children just coloured it in. Colouring in, which is a million miles away from thinking about colour and using it, is never education. Even worse, templates also provide a metaphor for thinking: should the children think in terms of the teacher's mental shapes, as well as draw inside the teacher's physical ones? All these things – felt tips, screwed-up tissue paper, templates, wax crayons – will, according to the Habitat and hessian school of thought, corrupt child and teacher alike. And biros …

Working with biros

On my third visit to Bealings, I went equipped with a bundle of cheap ballpoint pens. The cheapest are the best because they leave mucky little smudges. Often, when children begin working with them, they make no line at all. This leads to excited little scribbles as the child makes the paper bear the brunt of his fury. Sometimes, of course, you don't want mucky little lines, the equivalent of charcoal; you want clean, neat lines and then you will choose fine ballpoints. Another advantage ballpoint pens have over pencils is that the eraser is no longer an issue: an ink line cannot be rubbed out. Most important, you get an entirely different kind of line with a biro, as compared with a pencil, and its skinny look has a strength of its own in teaching children to draw.

Another point worth making here is that the children, once they have produced plenty of drawings, should be allowed to choose their graphic tools. In this book, I have given the children the tools I wanted them to use. This is not ideal, but it was necessary in my view for the book's production.

The subject of the ballpoint lesson was each child's right shoe. This served two useful purposes: first, it introduced the idea of the everyday as worthy subjects for art. George Herbert, the seventeenth-century priest and poet, wrote 'Who sweeps a room, as for [God's] laws, / Makes that and th'action fine' ('The Elixir', *Collected Poems* 176). Similarly, whoever looks at the most ordinary things with the eye of an artist 'until it hurts' makes the ordinary beautiful. Making the ordinary beautiful, or at least interesting – I think of this computer screen, and that stereo playing behind me as I type, and my desk lamp – is a duty for manufacturers in a literal sense, and a duty for artists in an extended sense. Also, manufacturers have a duty not to make things that are vulgar, but that have good design grafted onto them. They should make things in which the design is in an organic relationship to the function. The stereo is, indeed, a machine for listening to music. It should reflect that function by being as visually silent, so to speak, as possible. Artists have to make the ordinary beautiful for observers of their art. They are in the fortunate position of making what is ugly, beautiful.

How can horrible events in art be beautiful? This is not a difficult question to answer. Look at Goya's painting, *The Third of May* (1808), in the Prado, Madrid but reproduced widely. On the right, a phalanx of soldiers in tunics and boots, their faces hidden, aim guns at an unarmed man in a white shirt and gold trousers. His arms are spread wide. On his hands is blood: he looks like Jesus on the cross. Whether his arms are raised in surrender or protest it is impossible to say. Another man, blood flowing from him, lies in front of him. Other men seem to have been lined up for the firing squad. The next in line covers his face with his hands. The whole canvas is mostly dark browns and greys, except for the white-shirted man and a small area around him. In the background is what looks like a town with a prominent church.

The scene could not be more ugly. The painting could hardly be more beautiful. The artist who achieves this, without giving us the impression that he is a prurient observer, or a journalist, is a great artist. The artist who does not attempt to address the dark and the ugly is no artist at all. With children it is worth helping them to address at least the ordinarily ugly: car engines, building sites, worn shoes.

A second reason for the shoe lesson was that the ordinary objects surprised the children. The value of surprise in teaching seems to me to be increasingly important as I get older. More and more I admire the student teacher who began a creative writing lesson by entering the classroom with a coal scuttle on his head. When I try to think of examples of beginning lessons with a surprise, I feel ashamed that I can think of none.

To turn to the drawings: Olivia is now '10 in August', I note (Figure 3.1). Her habitual intensity was even more striking than usual. She never manages to do a large drawing, one that gets close to filling the page. Instead, with quiet concentration, she slowly builds her image. When I look at this drawing of her shoe, I try to work out how and why it moves me so much. It reminds me of Van Gogh's chair and his pipe (*The Yellow Chair with Pipe*, Tate Gallery, London). The great artist paints something about himself when he paints his chair; the child draws something about herself when she draws her shoe. It is a platitude that the possessions of a relative who has died – shoes, clothes, Bible, unused bottles of sauce – are what move us most. These children's intimate possessions move me here, too. The drawing is, as Read (1931: 33) writes, 'the clearest signature that the artist has left us'. When the objects are powerfully drawn, intimate objects, they are what Read again calls 'a complete realisation of a fragment of life – a fold of drapery, the profile of a face, the contour of a muscle, the structure of a flower ...' And we might add, the shape of a shoe.

When I look at Olivia's drawing I think also of the praying hands of Dürer and temporarily discarded objects in Vermeer: that basket, that book, and especially that cello in *The Concert* (Isabella Stewart Gardner Museum, Boston, USA). I note that she has kept hold of the instruction from the first session, that she has found many ways of using whatever graphic tool (in this case, of course, a biro) she is holding. Here, we can see cross-hatching, wiggly and curly lines, smudging, and delicate little arcs. Olivia (according to my notes) has almost nothing to offer verbally during lessons, either to me or to the other children. On her drawing, she has written unintentional doggerel: 'My shoe is old and torn / Wherever I go it's been worn.' She has arranged her writing in the shape of the shoe.

Lindsay's drawing (Figure 3.2) also confirmed what I knew about her already. In contrast to Olivia, she draws quickly and always with the same effect of a slight casualness, airiness and smudginess that I find attractive. I often look at Lindsay's drawings to find out what it is they remind me of. An openness to new ideas? A freedom? A confidence? She looks up at me as I praise her work. 'That's lovely, Lindsay.' 'I know', she replies. Sophie (Figure 3.3) writes 'My shoe is special because it can only fit my foot'.

Emily, as ever, is drawn quickly to vivid words as she draws (Figure 3.4): 'The shiny patches on my shoe remind me of the sun shining on a sparkling lake. The tiny sewing on my shoe reminds me of a troop of ants. The velcro reminds me of a long bushy beard. The shiny F reminds me of a hot glowing sun. The creases remind me of my old Grandma's wrinkled face.'

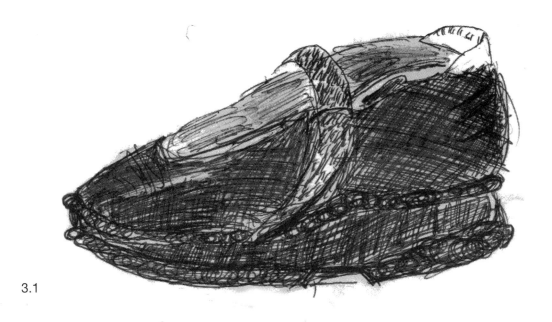

3.1

3.2

The other Key Stage 2 drawings offered me less insight so I have not reproduced them here. The Key Stage 1 children were unable to come to the lesson because they were undergoing a test. Real life kept intruding, and I had decided by now to let that human mess be a part of my book. Real life has its glories and its anxieties – I did not want my book to show some ideal, and therefore spurious, progress through a term in a perfect school unaffected by everyday life.

All rules are there to be broken: that art teaching should be planned is one and discard clichés is another. I broke both of them because, having some time left, I found a spider plant, which the children drew (Figures 3.5 to 3.8). I preferred to use the spare time with more drawing and although 'spider plants died out with Habitat and hessian' (as Andrea Durrant puts it), I was pleased with the results. All the

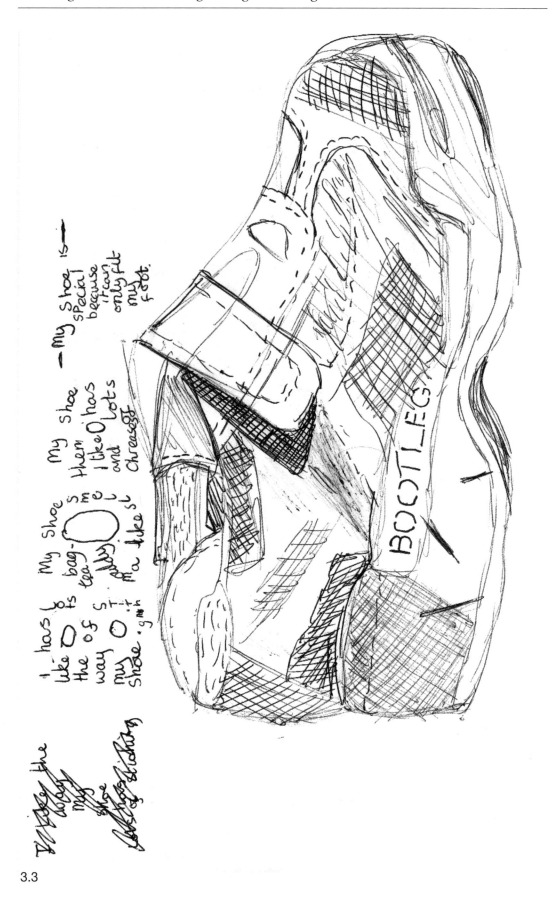

My Shoe

My shoe is special because it can only fit my feet.

My shoe is bag-teal them I like O and Lots of Threads

My shoe has O like the O of way O it ally my shoe. gmm

3.3

The shiny patches on my shoe remind me of the sun shining on a sparkling lake.
The tiny sewing on my shoe remind me of a troop of ants
The velcro Reminds me of a long bushy beard
The shiny (F) Reminds me of a hot glowing Sun.
The creases remind me of my old Grandmas wrinkled face.

3.4

3.5

3.6

children (especially Sophie, Olivia and Alex) appeared to relish the opportunity the plant gave them for sweeping movements of the hand. Most of the children augmented their biro lines with pencil, adding depth to their work. I liked the way Anna concentrated on the brown, straggly, less elegant leaves of the plant (Figure 3.7). There was no time for the children to write on their drawings.

In the next lesson, we needed something different. I thought about going outside and about movement. The Key Stage 1 children needed work to help them catch up and, Henry, among other Key Stage 1 children, needed some work to help him to draw with the same confidence and vigour that he brought to his task as a goalkeeper. I reflected on different graphic tools: charcoal, chalk, paint, ink and crayons. Drawing is not just a useful learning tool for its own sake or for the sake of the subject being closely observed and drawn – it is a basic element in all aspects of art and design. It is a medium for preparatory work in painting, sculpture and carving. Its position in the powerful middle ground – after and during thought, and before the production of work in other forms of visual art – makes it uniquely valuable as a discipline for artists of all ages. It has, of course, a vital place in sketchbooks, which are as indispensable in schools that take art seriously as notebooks are in schools that are serious about writing.

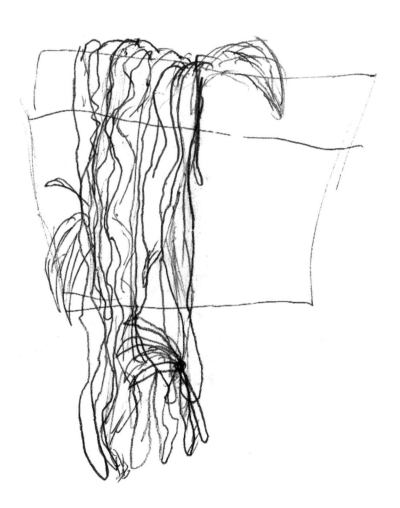

3.7

3.8

4 Felt Tips, and the Movement and the Anger

I rang Duncan, putting off a drawing date with the children. My life was busy, too, but no busier than anyone else's. I am irritated when people say how busy they are. They are boasting, and the only answer is to say 'Join the club'. So they've taken one child to ballet, another to football, stripped down the car engine and put it back together again, been to Calais to stock up on wine, decorated the dining room, prepared a dinner party, listened to the Schubert String Quintet and written a short story. All on a Saturday morning. Great. They forget how busy it is not being busy: studying racing form in *The Sporting Life*, or drinking strong cider on benches on the Town Hall steps, or gardening all weekend. I know for a fact that I would find all of these last three esoteric activities quite exhausting.

A note for a future lesson: draw yourself when you are busiest.

But I was working with secondary students on GCSE poetry, and with sixth-formers on *Othello*, and I was thinking about the differences and similarities between primary schools and their culture, and secondary schools and theirs. All this took up much of my professional space, of course, but to me at the time (and, still now) it felt like my emotional space too. The differences between secondary and primary will have to wait for another time, another place. But there is one similarity. Secondary students and teachers are bound by statutory requirements, as much (if not more) than primary students. There are examinations, obviously, like tests in primary schools.

But a more subtle official corruption is at work there. Certain poems – by Carol Anne Duffy, Simon Armitage and Fleur Adcock among others – are becoming official poems. I enjoyed almost all these prescribed poems that I had to teach: they weren't written 'officially', of course, they only became official when they were included in anthologies published by examination boards. But I have a special admiration for those writers who have refused to let their work take on any kind of official status in anthologies produced by the National Examinations and Assessment Board (NEAB 1998). The making of good poetry, like the making of all good art, is never official. It is the opposite. It is an attempt to show that we are human beings, not numbers on a checklist. Once it is made, official art places the human at a distance beyond a foreground of indisputable dogma. That is why commissioned architecture in great public spaces such as Trafalgar Square is always problematic. Although official art apparently aspires to the status of art, the very fact of its being official almost always cripples it. Look what has happened to successive Poets Laureate: all men, of course; and each one more or less emasculated by his search for poems about a new royal baby, or a wedding. Look at the unlamented Millennium Dome.

Officialdom tops its plinths in public places with warlords and politicians. Are these statues art? They may be, but they are something else first: the political insistence on the power of management. Officialdom has a worrying tendency to take over the representation of art in all schools as well:

> Those [pictures] presented in reproduction to the schools by the Sainsbury's Pictures for Schools Scheme are excellent, but they have become the only pictures that many children see ... All children now have the opportunity to see Two Boys and Girl Making Music, by Jan Molenaer, The Woodman's Daughter by John Millais, Child with Dove by Picasso and Orthodox Boys by Bernard Perlin ... The pictures have been disempowered by their becoming official. They have become ornaments ... (Sedgwick 2001:6)

When I got round to making a date with Bealings it was another unreliable spring day. I had spent the first part of it busily sorting out normal problems: a sick cat, a very sick car steaming under the bonnet (a wife not too well either), a nagging accountant, a set of proofs from a publisher to be returned within the month. By the time of my arrival, during mid-afternoon, it was playtime. Duncan had arranged for most of the children to be dressed, as I had requested, for a PE lesson.

The older ones arrived in the PE/assembly hall, by now standing in as our studio. They wore T-shirts, shorts or jeans, and trainers. I showed them the chisel-nibbed felt tip pens that I had bought earlier that afternoon, and then talked about the two kinds of line that they could make: one thin, one fat. I suggested, pretty strongly, that the felt tips would not work very well for heavy shading. I didn't want to take home a sheaf of featureless black shapes. Duncan had supplied us with large sheets of paper, which I tore in half, and a variety of other felt tip pens.

I asked the children to run around the room, making sure they did not bump into each other. When I clapped they were to make a star shape, 'stretching every muscle, including the muscles of their fingers and their feet'. We tried this a few times. They ran again, and at my clap they were to make 'a hedgehog shape' ('any parts sticking out I will come and tread on!'). After another run, I asked the children to balance on one leg with arms stretched one way or the other; then, again, to choose whichever one of the physical shapes they had tried that they liked. As this was going on, the younger children drifted in, looking understandably puzzled, still clad in full school uniform. I asked them to get ready to join the dance, and they did. The things we ask children to do! The way they do them, gladly!

All this was made up of a PE lesson I had taught during my first teaching practice in 1965. I trained at a college where physical education was highly valued, and, although I was generally unsympathetic to the pervading PE hegemony, I learned much from it that came in useful when I was a young teacher. The children ran, stopped, star-shaped, balanced, rolled over into tight shapes. They arrived quickly at the state where they were breathing heavily. By now all the younger ones had turned up, and when they stopped, six-year-old Alistair lay on the floor with a 'Phew!' There were some pleasingly red faces around the hall. As well as their drawing, I was thinking about the children's health. Research has suggested that children rarely get their heartbeat up to a level beneficial to their hearts even once in a day. These had, I thought, looking at them.

As soon as the children were lying and sitting around the hall, chests heaving, apparently exhausted – and, in some cases, it seemed, near to death – I asked them to choose one of the positions that they had found in their brief PE lesson, and to draw it. I felt that although they had not seen their bodies as they moved, they would have felt the effects of their movement. Also, they had seen each other. This was not just art education; it was, obviously, health education and also physical education. But the children were also learning about the science of the human body by intensifying their experience of that body: arguably a firsthand experience worth having before theoretical study with textbooks.

Two of the older children produced work that was less interesting than pictures they had drawn before. Indeed (as will emerge even more clearly in this chapter) the older Key Stage 2 children were putting less into lessons than they had at the start of the project. Perhaps Alex, for example, was becoming bored with the project: we were now well into May and leaving primary school was on the horizon. I worried about them, not so much for their own sakes, but because of the effect this decline might have on my book: one kind of professionalism (concerned with my writing) was putting another, arguably more important kind (concerned with my teaching) into the shade. The youngest children, Alistair and William especially, produced stick figures not worth reproducing.

Alex's conventional piece of work, also not reproduced here, was a figure with a big grin but no sense of movement. Sophie, too (I have not put her drawing in, either) made a static image, and she drew the eyes as two dots as though she had forgotten the 'Look, look, look' rule (which I had recapped: look at what your body must look like …). Emily's figure (Figure 4.1) was stronger. Although she has written 'I felt energetic and funny about standing on one leg', it seems to be airbound.

But Olivia (Figure 4.2) is always extraordinary. She is, to use a casual and unhelpful phrase, a natural artist: not in the conventional sense, but in the sense (perhaps this is part of the conventional sense) that she does what she pleases. She takes on the teaching around her insofar as she feels or thinks she needs it, but still does her own thing. It will be interesting to see what happens if she makes something that, to my eye, fails. In conversation, she was more outgoing on this occasion than she had ever been before – freed, perhaps by her PE clothes. Or maybe she was in justifiable extravert reaction to the end of SATs week. I showed her the first drawing she had done with me. Although she agreed that her work was getting better, she said: 'I still like my sleeping cat.' An artist should have the confidence to stand up for what she has done.

Her drawings always bear examination. On this occasion, she has captured her flowing hair and the instability of the pose in her first piece. I had told the children that, if they wore their hair long, they should note the feeling of it as it played behind them, and record that feeling in their drawings. Children are very able at this kind of detail, once the importance of it has been pointed out to them. I said to Olivia: 'You

I felt stretched out like a flammingo on one leg, on a balle
I felt energetic and funny about standing on one leg

4.1

I am runing in different diretions like a mouse wanting to get out of a cage.

4.2

I am standing on one leg like a flamingo. My head and arms are facing the floor. I am letting my arm sway.

super star shape !
I felt like a acrobatic super star!

4.3

have drawn this with great care, haven't you? Now draw yourself in a different position with the same care.' She was very amused by this second drawing, as I am. What is it that makes this drawing so true and so funny? I wish now that I had suggested that she drew herself in other positions. I would then have in front of me a sheet of paper redolent of learning resembling those pages of Leonardo's in his notebooks. I could have captioned it 'Olivia works towards understanding her body as it runs and jumps and crawls.' Under the first drawing she wrote a phrase about a flamingo that other children later copied, and then she wrote: 'I am running in different directions like a mouse wanting to get out of a cage.'

I am beginning to think that the white space that Olivia always leaves around her drawings – in spite of instructions that the children should draw their subject 'close-up' – is important to her. This space is a vital element in her drawings. It is part of the meaning of what she is trying to convey. Looking through my collection of art postcards I can see how eloquent space is in any painting by Edward Hopper (see Renner 1990 for many examples). Or I look at a card of a reproduction of Jan Vermeer's great picture *Girl with a Pearl Earring* (Mauritshuis, The Hague). How much less of a picture it would be without all that grey-black darkness to the left of the girl's face. What does it tell us? Something about the gloom that surrounds this lovely girl. Even the pictures in the Pileta caves use space articulately. And you cannot look at architecture without thinking about space: its wide rectangles of white, the expanses of sky (whatever colour it might be).

Another curious aspect of these two drawings is that Olivia has, very unusually for children, chosen to draw herself so that her face cannot be seen. Perhaps the space and the lack of face are connected. Olivia is doing what all artists have to do, which is to tell the story of her psyche, knowingly or not, in her work; to tell the story of her soul; or to hint at it. As Edwards (1992:23) says, 'the more clearly you can see and draw what you see in the external world, the more clearly the viewer can see you, and the more you can know about yourself'. This applies, it seems to me, even when – or especially when – we are drawing ourselves. If Olivia has secretive tendencies, her art will show them. She will look away from the camera, sometimes, not at it. 'As with the Zen master-archer the target is yourself' (Edwards 1992:23).

Anna, who is nine, always conscientiously preserves her wrong lines. She keeps this rule more than the other children, and seems happier with it than they are. She never turns the paper over, that traditional ritual of the schoolchild, to start again, as some of the other children do. Note here (Figure 4.3) the line across the face down the right eye (as we look at the picture). As she drew this, she realised that she wanted her drawing to be bigger. And look at the trouser leg on the left of the drawing. The first line is more static than the second. It had obviously been worth asking her to do the little burst of PE: 'Super star shape! I felt like a[n] acrobatic superstar!' She had not drawn the figures on her T-shirt very carefully until I pointed out to her that the legs on the figures on the shirt had legs that had shape – they were not just single lines – and that they were holding ski-ing gear. The little drawings got stronger. It is nearly always worth presenting children with small graphic problems when you are dissatisfied with what they have done. Give them 'another hurdle'. This was advice that a romantic novelist told me was always given to others of his kind when things were not going well. Put some obstacle in the way of your characters is what I believe he meant. Getting your characters over that obstacle will test your narrative skills. In my terms, in drawing lessons, it means presenting the children with another challenge. Because Anna is so biddable, this always leads to interesting developments in her work.

After she read an early draft of my book, my wife made a suggestion. I mapped it out as lesson notes for September when I was due to see most of these children again:

Ask one child to freeze in a pose: all limbs stretched, for example, like in the famous Leonardo image. Get the children to draw their model in that pose – quickly, with all the four rules of drawing in mind (no erasers, close-up, different pencil marks, keep looking). After a few minutes, make him adopt a different pose. (Bending over to one side, limbs still stretched? Think yoga.) Ask the children to draw him in that new pose, on top of their first drawings – in a different kind of graphic tool? Other poses: hedgehog. Squatting. Repeat until everyone is fed up.

And come September, I did this lesson. Last April seemed a long time ago, with the summer intervening. The school was its usual bustle of activity, but I noticed that normal September quietness that contrasts so much with the demob-happy high jinks of the weeks of July. Two of the children – Rosemary and Anna – didn't turn up. They were working on a computer, finding Maori artwork. Also, of course, my Year 6 friends had left to go to secondary school.

First, I refreshed the children's memory of the many kinds of line lesson from the first chapter. Then Alistair posed: first on tiptoe with his legs spread and his fingers 'reaching for the sky'; second, bending sideways at the trunk, arms on his waist; and third, hunkered down like a footballer posing for a photograph with the ball between his knees. He had to relax every minute or so. As he posed, and as I changed his pose, the children drew as fast as they could, continually looking at their model. I can find little more to say about Olivia, who at last, as she writes on her drawing, is now '10!' Here (Figure 4.4) is the usual terrific intensity, the total confidence with the pencil and what she can do with it. Olivia always draws well, and when I look at her earlier drawings, I find it hard to see any development. That second cat (p. 25) is as strong as this drawing. Henry, on the other hand, who began this course uncertainly (though desperate to learn and to do well, and always with almost old-fashioned courtesy that encouraged me when things were not going as well as I had anticipated: thanks, Henry) has developed his drawing to the point where he was as little fazed as Olivia by this task. Even his second cat last April was a wooden little creature (p. 27) (though much stronger than his first one); now, his Alistair visibly stretches, looking a little like an angel, then bends, and then crouches (Figure 4.5).

I once got into an argument in the columns of the *Times Educational Supplement* with a director of a manufacturing firm who complained that schools were failing, and it was all so simple, really: education was (in his horrible phrase) 'a routine batch exercise'. Olivia and Henry stand for me as a vivid and eloquent refutation of that kind of thinking. Children come to us in many conditions. Intellectually, they might be ready to stand apparently still and consolidate their present position. Or they might be ready to shoot suddenly ahead, only to come to a position of consolidation

I had to draw Alister in three diferent positions on top of each other
7/9/01
10!

4.4

4.5

4.6

farther down the road. Sometimes they will seem to fail, and often that is when the most powerful learning happens, or perhaps when the most powerful learning is about to happen: as they walk away, wondering what went wrong.

Jeremy's drawing (Figure 4.6) is mature: his attack is vigorous, and the image has few of the symbolic elements one might expect in a piece by a child so young. Indeed, he carefully analyses his subject and doesn't seem bothered by the difficult and complicated nature of the task.

Then William posed in the first two positions of a sprinter's Ready, Steady, Go. Here are Olivia's, Jeremy's and Henry's drawings (Figures 4.7, 4.8, 4.9). Henry writes proudly: 'It was really hard getting everything in position. But I managed the task.'

Because there was time left, I asked the children to draw Lindsay (who is small) and Olivia (who is tall) posing in a play fight, and I include Jeremy's drawing here (Figure 4.10).

This session lasted only three quarters of an hour, but I felt encouraged by it.

The anger

That was later. On the same day (July) that I taught the first movement lesson, I talked to the children about anger. 'What makes you angry?' The children told me stories about moments when they felt that they had been treated unfairly: 'When my Mummy doesn't let me play my game boy … When my sister jumps on me … When my brothers wake me up in the middle of the night …' I asked the children, 'What do you feel inside your heads, inside your hearts when you are angry? What shapes do you feel?' After these questions, I then asked the children to close their eyes, to cover them with their hands, and think. There is rarely enough time in primary schools for thought. There is too much noise and too much waving to gain attention. Nothing happens intellectually, emotionally or spiritually as children stick their arms in the air, impatiently waving their hands, often calling 'Yes!' or 'Sir!' or 'Me!' By contrast, in the silences we can offer children, much unrecordable work is done, and, for many of the children, much welcome peace is experienced. This work is undervalued by officials simply because it is difficult, or even impossible, to place on checklists. They are obsessed with '[taking] a metre rule / to measure the sublime / measureless universe', to use Geoffrey Hill's lovely words from his translation of Ibsen's play *Brand* (1978, quoted in Milne 1998).

Also, it is often forgotten (if the displays in some excellent schools are to be trusted) that drawing lessons should sometimes be concerned with subjects that cannot be dealt with simply by slow, deliberate observation. Read (1931:32) writes that, while some drawings (most, probably) aim at the 'accurate and exacting study of some detail', other drawings record the 'sudden flash of vision'. I would add that this sudden flash need not necessarily be a vision of what is visual to the outer eye. Sometimes it is about what can only be seen with 'the mind's eye'. In this lesson, the children try to observe and express in a rapid way their gut feelings about something that has moved them deeply.

The older children's drawings were uniformly dull and random, shapeless scribbles all over the page. Perhaps they were tired after the SATs. The thought

we drew william
in Ready 𝘀 stedy

4.7

The race

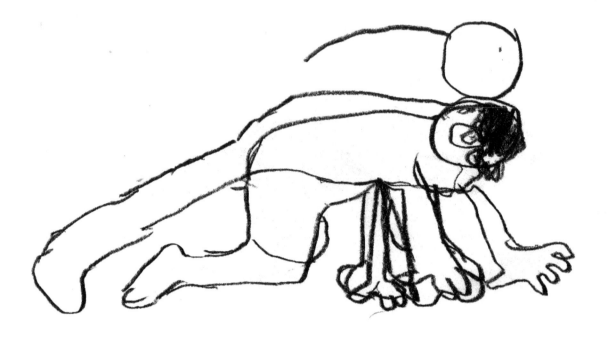

It was fun.

4.8

ready, steady GO!

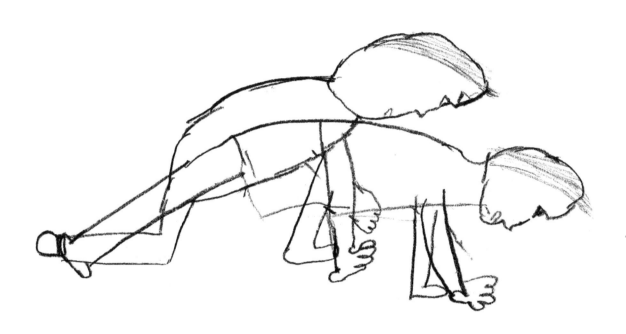

it was really hard getting everthing in
position. But i managed the tesk

4.9

I was fun drawing Pople fighting.

4.10

occurred: should I challenge them next time about this? In contrast, the younger children all produced interesting drawings. Sam, who had turned up for the first time, had made movement drawings that were uninteresting. He had not taken on board any of my rules because he did not know them. Surprised at the nature of the task, he drew stick men. He was, as far as I am concerned, part of the world that is troubled with a lack of looking. He used a symbol of a man, rather than an image that was connected to close observation.

But see his anger. His drawing (Figure 4.11) is as controlled as one of those graphs that records heartbeats, with knife points where the heartbeats reach panic level, and a calmer area before and afterwards. His sentence says '[I am angry] when my brother hits me.' Is there a connection with the heartbeats Sam and I gleefully stimulated earlier in the PE lesson and this drawing? Is there some mysterious spark leaping between the actual beating heart and the representation of it on an electronic screen, and then on a piece of paper? (Sam never turned up again.)

Jeremy gets angry 'when my sister jumps on me' (Figure 4.12) and his drawing too is controlled, like the image some of us get from a classic migraine. Alistair's lines (Figure 4.13), also controlled and purposeful, led to writing that gives us a glimpse into domestic life (he has three younger brothers, including twins): 'When my brothers wake me up in the night it makes me very really angry because they cry. Then I have to go into there (*sic*) room and sing them a song.' William's curly lines (Figure 4.14) look like skeins of smoke floating up over mountainsides from the valleys of Hell. One of them becomes a complicated and threatening cloud. He gets angry 'when my Mummy doesn't let me play my game boy'.

Why were the juniors so much less successful on this occasion? They had just finished a week during which they had been subjected to their SATs. But perhaps younger children, being closer to the clouds of glory from which they came, are simply better at abstract drawing, at drawing what their feelings are. In Margaret Morgan's formulation (Morgan 1988), they are still more symbolist than analytical, and therefore more able to represent emotions than to analyse facts visually.

Later, Andrea Durrant showed me another way of drawing feelings. I asked the children to write the name of a feeling on the back of a piece of paper: cheerful, angry, excited, gloomy, sad. They were then to make marks to try to convey that emotion. The children had to guess what each other's drawing depicted.

The summer came. I didn't see any of the children, or Bealings Primary School itself, for what seemed like a long time. I continued with my day job: writer in schools, jobbing poet. I worked on an anthology of poems, wrote occasional journalism, and obsessively went over the drawings I had collected from Bealings and earlier drafts of my commentary on them. I sent these drafts to various colleagues who commented on them, helpfully or unhelpfully, kindly or unkindly. The children got on with their science and music, their literacy and their maths. Henry, I heard, was on a goalkeeping course with a Premiership club. There was talk of my going to St Ives the following summer to be a writer-in-residence with the children in the Hepworth garden and in the Tate Gallery. That kept me going.

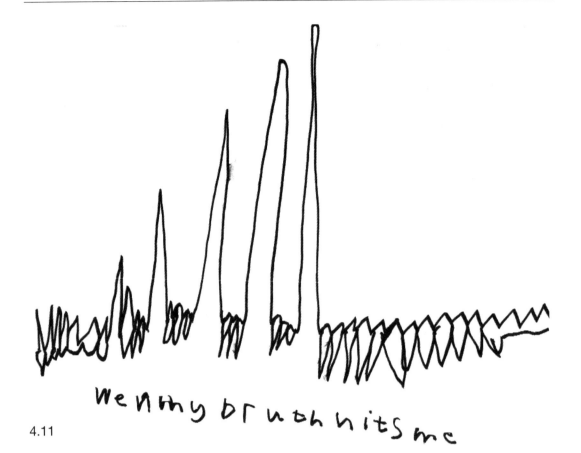

wen my bruth hits me

4.11

What makes me angrey is when
my sister Jumps on me.

4.12

When my brothers wake
up in the night it
makes me very realy angry.
becaese they cry
Then I have to go into there
room and sing them a song

4.13

4.14

5 Drawing Blind and Drawing Outside

Drawing blind

About four weeks had passed since the last session and we were well into June. Some of the Year 6 children had seemed less committed to the project than they had been at the beginning. This was, first, perhaps, because they were what teachers call at this time of the year 'demob-happy'. As the secondary school on the edge of town – Ipswich for these village children – loomed, with its potential for achievement and distress, with its rumours and reputation, and with its sheer size, the little primary school and its projects like mine must have appeared less significant than 'they had seemed earlier. The family-like pleasures of a school such as Bealings must have begun to seem out of date to the children: in their word, uncool.

Second, the children were – like the teachers, like me, like everyone working in education – tired. Often teachers feel their own sense of exhaustion at the end of the summer term without considering that the children might be feeling something similar. I was teaching in schools in a glazed way, looking forward to the Greek island where we had booked our holiday; but I didn't give a moment's thought to how the children might be feeling – until I sat down to write these notes.

And, third, connected with this, some of the children had been on a school trip to Paris. A drawing club is small beer compared to climbing the Eiffel Tower and visiting an art gallery, much as any school (even Bealings) was becoming small beer to me, compared to Lesvos, and its fetta and retsina, its beaches and its castles, its monasteries and its petrified forest. And finally, on this last occasion when I was to work with the Year 6 children, they were looking forward to their outing to a Kentucky Fried Chicken restaurant with Duncan and some of their parents.

I felt that it was time for experiments. First, I asked the children to draw some objects that they could not see, but that they could feel. Andrea Durrant had given me this idea on a course we had taught together a fortnight before. I use a similar idea when I am teaching writing. For example, I ask children to close and cover their eyes, and imagine a box inside their heads (Sedgwick 1997). In this, I deprive children of all their senses in order to help them to intensify the use of their memory and imagination.

With Durrant's idea, we deprive children of their sense of sight in order to intensify the use of their tactile sense. Often depriving ourselves of one sense intensifies the use that we make of the others: imagine, for example, looking at pictures in a gallery with our hearing shut out, or listening to music in the dark. Both activities should be tried at least once. In the first instance, the seeing will be intensified; in the second the hearing.

I hid, among other things, a necklace, a ceramic pot and a large fir cone inside plastic bags. Only three of the drawings were worth reproducing. This was because the session proved a considerable challenge to the children, and because I was teaching this lesson for the first time and hadn't prepared it properly. I felt that I was guilty of a kind of arrogance here: I had found this terrific lesson, and therefore it should work in this school. Sophie (Figure 5.1) probably had the easiest task as the necklace presented no problems of tactile identification. She wrote her last sentence after the lesson, when she had taken the necklace out of the bag. Lindsay's fir cone drawing has her customary vigour and was drawn with her customary speed. It has a lovely, almost abstract, quality. It reminds me of a rough sketch of some Mediterranean village, all roofs seen from a nearby hill. The Cézanne of *Village Seen Through Trees* (Kuntshalle, Bremen) and many other paintings would have been interested in this drawing (Figure 5.2). Emily's drawing of a pot is also typical of her style: painstaking and conscientious (Figure 5.3).

Drawing outside

Drawing outside hardly constitutes an experiment, but it was new to this project. After the last session, I took the children onto the playground and suggested familiar objects that they might draw. These included a shelter that the children used when it rained at playtime; bushes and trees; shelves under windows, the windows themselves reflecting horizontal Venetian blinds; part of the wall where there was (to me, anyway) an attractive contrast between the smoothness of an air vent and the roughness of the surrounding brickwork. All these things fell into that category of the everyday that is made interesting if we look until it hurts; those things that we do not know at all until we draw them, or, in my case, write about them.

The children ignored most of the objects that I suggested and drew objects that I would not have bothered with. Sophie, for example, chose a numbered snake shape painted on the playground by adults interested in giving children things to play with (Figure 5.4). I was, at first, disappointed by her choice. The snake has no third dimension, of course, and it is, to my eye, boring. But she came to this object, and the drawing of it, with a much more interesting baggage than I had. Thus she taught me a lesson that I have been taught a thousand and more times, and which I have still not learned: do not dismiss what you can't immediately see any value in. Sophie had played on this shape, schoolday after schoolday, for six years (an eternity for her). Therefore it held potent memories. She makes a lovely page of her work. She writes: 'There are lots of small cracks where ants could fall into.' She then moves, at my suggestion, into reminiscence:

On the snake I have played What's the time Mr Wolf. I never used to do very well and I was always eaten by the wolf. I have also played a lot of hopscotch on it but

It has a wire through the middle.
I think its a necklace
It has a silver fastner.
It's green with white crosses.

5.1

It feels ruff

5.2

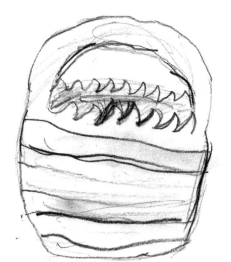

A pot with decorative green leaves on it. It feels smooth

5.3

am drawing part of the snake on the playground. The texture is very bumpy and nobbly. The numbers are blue and the snake is yellow. The play grounds is a greyey black and it has lots of white stones in Their are lots of small gracks where ants could fall into.

on the snake I have played 'Whats the time Mr wolf' I never used to do very well and I was allways eaten by the wolf have allso played a kind of hop scotch on it but it never really worked. When I was little I used to skip alolong the snake and think I was g ~~through~~ on the snakes back and pretend it was to slithering across the soggy jungle floor

5.4

it never really worked. When I was little I used to skip along the snake and think I was riding on the snake's back and pretend it was slithering across the soggy jungle floor ...

I would never have seen these little pictures of Sophie's earlier childhood if she had not drawn the snake. Nor would I have seen them if I conceived of visual art as so precious that it should not be contaminated by words. Looking at her picture now, I think that had I been more alert to learning possibilities, I should have suggested that she might place a frame around part of the surface of the playground. She could then have concentrated on conveying to a viewer as much as she could about the texture and appearance of that square, with all my earlier suggestions about pencil marks in mind. I was not having a good morning: my bland assumption about the possible success of the 'feely' lesson had been proved wrong, and now I had missed a chance to teach.

Lindsay scurried off in her characteristic manner, and, characteristically again, produced a vivid, hurried drawing of the gate (Figure 5.5). I am tempted to write (and will give way to the temptation, as is my way), that it is the essence of 'gate'. It is similar to her drawing of the fir cone (p. 85). Both are rough drawings of 'ruff' subjects. Emily and Olivia still seemed to me to be committed to the project. Emily, who was about to leave the school, asked me how she would be able to find this book. She always takes seriously whatever I suggest. She drew the hollyhocks with faint lines (Figure 5.6), and then emphasised the edges of the bricks with stronger lines. I suggested that this made the bricks look more important than the flowers. She agreed, and strengthened the outlines of the flowers. I am not sure that my intervention made for an improvement. It is always such a delicate matter, when to say something, what to say, when to say nothing. Teachers face profoundly educational decisions every moment of their professional lives. In the current climate, you might think that all the decisions are made in planning and record-keeping. This is not so. It is the action in the classroom that counts, not the detached poring over tables and planning sheets on Sunday afternoons that should be spent in the park or the garden, on the beach or up a mountain ...

Olivia drew with her usual tenseness (Figure 5.7). I asked her if she drew at home. 'Cartoons' she replied. I told her, a bit snootily, that I was not interested in cartoons. Her drawing is strong, and she too has used memory in her notes: 'someone climbed this ledge to see what was happening in the reception classroom and they got told off. I was in Year 4.' I have to reflect here that Olivia's drawing, strong as it is, might be stronger if she had a wider choice of pencil. The last drawing (Figure 5.8) here is anonymous, another rough piece that may have turned the artist off hollyhocks for life: 'I don't like hollyhocks because they are difficult to draw.'

The climbing frame: the spaces between things

In the hall at Bealings Primary School, there is, of course, a wall-mounted climbing frame. A week later, I asked the older children to imagine a Martian who had never seen one and to report to this being what it looked like, purely by drawing. I suggested

11th July Lindsay age 7

the gate
It feals rummpy ruff and

5.5

Holly hocks next to bricks.

5.6

this is a very old ledge under these bits there are cobwebs. Someone climbed this ledge to see what was happening in the receptions class rooms and they got told off. I was in yr 4 at the time and I had just started Bealings.

5.7

These are
Hoy Hoes
11.7 01
Age 8

I dont Like HayHoks
Becose They are difcolt to draw

5.8

that they might do this, if they wanted, by concentrating not on the frame itself, but on the spaces between parts of the frame. The children had a choice of graphic tool: I had brought from home felt tips, pencils of various kinds, and ballpoints.

I like this kind of work because it blurs the common sense (and therefore untrustworthy) distinction between abstract and figurative drawing. Almost universally accepted as the only wise way of seeing things, common sense is in fact limiting and prejudiced. It was common sense, for example, in Victorian schools, to put dim pupils in a corner with dunce caps on their heads. It is common sense today to judge schools by statistics on bits of paper, rather than on the quality of the experiences children and teachers have within those schools. It is common sense to see art as either figurative or abstract. Anyone, like my Martian, who had never seen a climbing frame would be hard put to tell whether these drawings depicted objects or some shape conjured up by the artists' imaginations.

Using a ballpoint pen, Henry produced what was probably his best drawing of the term (Figure 5.9). It took about 20 minutes. He wrote his kind comment on it ('I like drawing this term with Fred ... I hope the Martian knows what it is') and the other children copied him. Sophie managed to capture in her drawing both the planes: the part of the frame facing her, and the other, drifting away in perspective on the right (Figure 5.10). Olivia, Emily and Lindsay worked in their characteristic ways (Figures 5.11, 5.12 and 5.13). Emily's drawing looks genuinely abstract; Lindsay's has her usual rushed vigour.

I used to have a pamphlet on my shelves (which I have lost) by Mary Newland and Maurice Rubens that was the inspiration for this lesson – and for much of the thinking in this book. They had asked children to draw a climbing frame, and to write on their paper alongside (or inside, or anywhere on) their drawings. One child had written a sentence that I have never forgotten. Surprised at the complicated image she had produced, and still (presumably) tired mentally because of the effort of observation and recording her observation, she had noted: 'This piece of art is not a lie.' The poet Wendy Cope said: 'When a poem doesn't work, the first question to ask yourself is "Am I telling the truth?"' This is true of all art, and as I look through the drawings I have collected during the course of producing this book, I am impressed by the children's vigilant search for truths about what they are drawing and writing about. This is especially relevant, I reflect now (at this late stage, preparing my typescript for Duncan's last look, and the publisher's approval), when the challenges the children have faced have been the most difficult: the cat only seen inside the head, the human figure in different positions, and (complicated, and not, on the face of it, remotely beautiful) the climbing frame.

The summer arrived at last. I flew to Lesvos with my family, Duncan to Cape Cod with his; I ate 20 or more Greek salads and loads of tsatziki; got sunburnt; drunk, twice; studied oleander, fig trees and palms, almost until it hurt; clowned around in the swimming pool; wrote an obscene limerick; walked around monasteries, saw a petrified forest; danced in the Greek manner as badly as it has ever been done before (and was photographed doing so). What the children did is not recorded. Some of them will, no doubt, have spent time in town, buying official school uniforms from the shops that had been shouting BACK TO SCHOOL in their display windows from 27 July onwards.

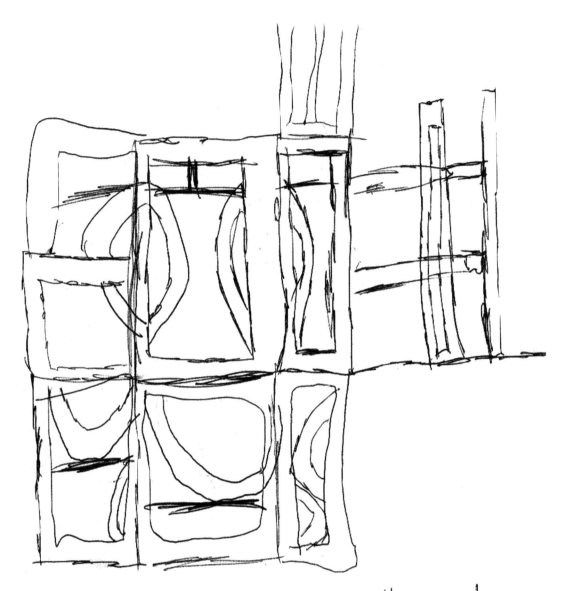

I liked Drawing ths term with Fred
It was really intresting
A hope the martian knows what it is.

5.9

I like drawing the climbing frame because it was quite complicated I really enjoyed coming to drawing club Thank you Fred.

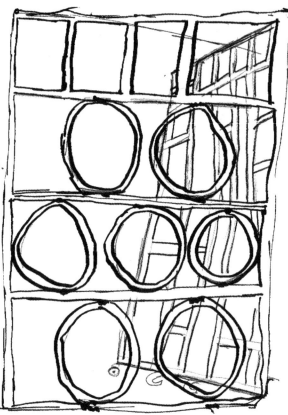

5.10

5.11

5.12

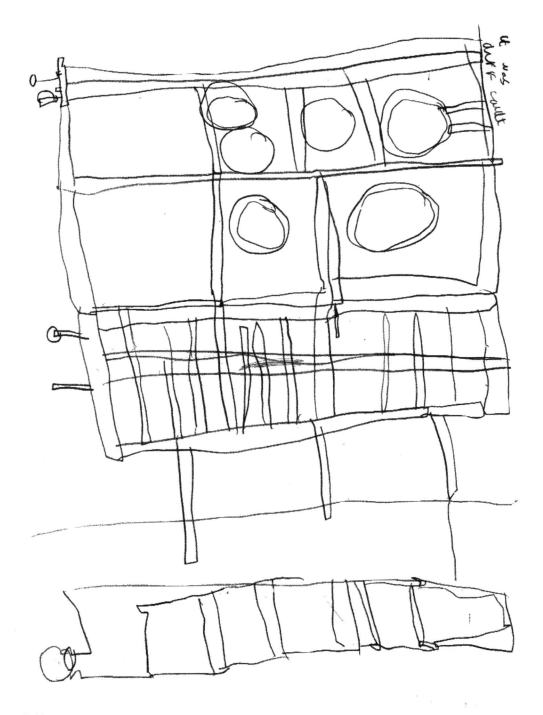

5.13

6 Further Ideas

Part 1

During the autumn I reflected on what I had missed out from my book. As a result, I wrote this last chapter, which is made up of two parts. The first is a list (with some illustrations) of further ideas for children's drawing. Some of the items in this list are no more than a comment on something that I have not done, but which I would have done if I'd had more time. There are other items, though, which I have taught. This supplementary list is not to be taken as evidence that I do not believe that there are many other ways of getting children drawing that are educational. If a book can be interactive, I would like to see evidence of it in the form of ideas sent to me: there is (as any honest writer will admit) an invisible list here of ideas that are not yet lit up in my brain and practice. A book on drawing – a book on anything – is, like a poem, never finished, only abandoned (Paul Valery, quoted in Auden 1971).

The second element in this chapter is made up of some tentative conclusions about learning and evaluation.

Drawing inspired by poetry

In western European culture, apart from the occasional actor who writes a novel, and the occasional poet who writes art criticism, conventionally there has been a separation between the arts. In other cultures, though, a sculptor might be, for example, both drummer and poet. The Nigerian Emmanuel Jegede, about whom I have written (Sedgwick 1988, 1989) used to talk to me about carving, drumming, painting and poetry all in one sentence. He was all of these, and was affectionately mystified at the grid western Europeans place on education (and, by extension, art). One result of the western European attitude is that we can (if we are not vigilant) lay waste the richness that can inform education if we do not appreciate that the arts feed each other. This is especially true, in my experience, of poetry and drawing. For an eccentric example of drawing and poetry co-existing on the page, and feeding each other, see the poems of Stevie Smith (1975) and Shel Silverstein (1974, 1982, among others).

Poetry and drawing is the only example I offer here of the correlation between the way the arts are linked. 'When I was a boy' (about bath times on the Isle of Wight) is an engaging poem from *Collected Poems for Children* by Charles Causley (1996), which I have been reciting to children for a decade. I said it to a group of six-year-olds and we discussed their own bath times. The purpose of this lesson is to get the children drawing vigorously from their memories, with more detail than such subjects usually inspire. If you merely instruct children to draw a picture called 'Bath time', they will produce a dull shape of a bath, probably small, and put themselves and some water in it. Causley's poem provides plenty of detail of a bath time in a working-class home at the beginning of the twentieth century: six children queuing, Mummy coming in with more hot water, water everywhere, 'soap on the ceiling', a scrubbing brush. I persuade the children to provide details from their own experiences, and they readily talk about toys, towels, steam, the toilet, fun, naughtiness.

Jack was a quiet boy who was usually (his teachers told me) reluctant to talk. This turned out to be an invigorating lesson for him. As he drew he became talkative, and a learning support assistant wrote down his words: 'My shark is very dangerous, very prickly and very bad, and very cross, with sharp teeth, with a big tail. There are fins on his back. He will bite your bottom. And his eyes' (Figure 6.1).

Jack has enclosed everything inside the shape of the bath, including a child with a heavily drawn navel, two demonic sharks, and carefully observed taps labelled 'h' and 'c'. The chain with the plug on the end of it seems to be flying off into the air.

Time and again I have found that drawing has an important function in freeing children who find words difficult. In Paine (1981) there is a chapter on Nadia Chomyn by Lorna Self. Nadia is described as a child who is 'suffering from autism … but with outstanding drawing ability'. I do not want to go into psychological theory here, having neither the qualifications to do so nor sufficient trust in the discipline as it impacts on schools. It is enough to say that Nadia's very low verbal abilities and her inability to communicate in conventional ways are in amazing contrast to her ability to draw. Perhaps in less extreme cases, other children are able to use in their drawing abilities that are hidden when they are restricted to purely verbal means of communication.

Paine's book will teach any alert reader much about the drawing of children, containing, as it does, work done in childhood by Millais and Toulouse-Lautrec, as well as drawings by gifted young people working at the end of the twentieth century. Margaret Morgan's chapter on David Downes' drawings sheds further light on what I have written about Nadia Chomyn: '[David] had severe difficulties in communicating in the normal way and in showing responses to other people. His co-ordination was very poor and at three years old he was unable to talk' (Morgan, quoted in Paine 1981).

David Downes developed an interest in buildings, houses, windmills, but especially churches. I have often taught children who had what psychologists thought were 'odd obsessions': the London Underground, car engines, ferries. Drawing is important for everybody because we all have difficulties at some time or another. It seems to me that we all might use this art to find, develop and learn from an obsession.

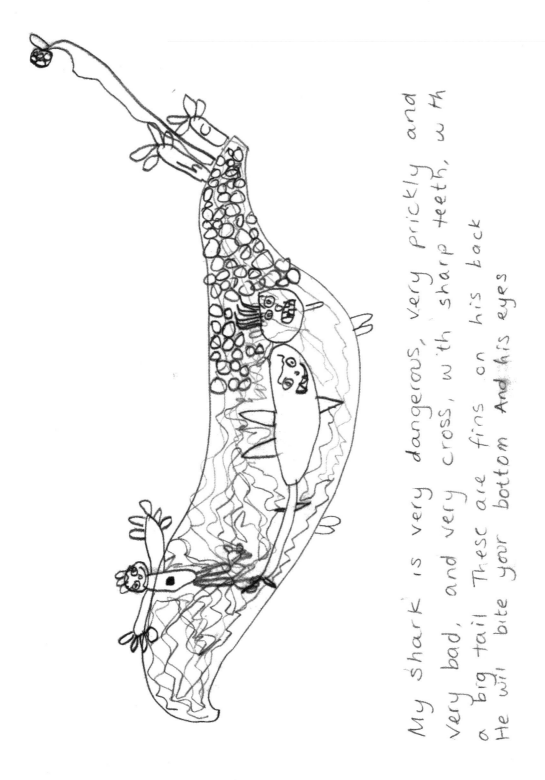

My shark is very dangerous, very prickly and
very bad, and very cross, with sharp teeth, wth
a big tail These are fins on his back
He wil bite your bottom And his eyes

6.1

Later, I tried the bath time idea with five- and six-year-old children at Bealings (Figures 6.2 and 6.3). I include here Kellie's steamy, bubbly bath with its ducks and Felicity's packed bathroom: 'This is my brother in the bath with his clothes on. My rubber duck is big.' You can find here, if you have the patience, in the manner of a child studying a *Where's Wally?* book, a rubber sponge, a mirror, Mummy saying 'Who's coming out next, this is my towel', and me (the bearded one). Look at both children's careful drawings of the chain that holds the plug. The strength of these drawings derives from discussion of such details before the drawing is started. I asked, for example, 'Can you show me with your finger how a chain's links are held together?' This discussion has led to other details that the children would otherwise have ignored: steam, the exact depiction of taps, the sponge. Looking hard at details like this makes children aware of design; at how the manufactured world works. We are not just teaching drawing: we are teaching technology.

I often use poems to get this kind of drawing. All this requires is lively verse, a subject matter familiar to the children and strong visual imagery. Here is a short list of poems suitable for getting children drawing, with references to anthologies:

- 'I remember' by Thomas Hood. This poem could lead to vivid recollection and drawing when used in conjunction with the four rules (p. 14). It can be found in many anthologies, including Mitchell 1993 and my own collection *Will there Really be a Morning?* (2002).

- 'Pied Beauty' by Gerard Manley Hopkins. This poem would provide opportunities to draw any elements from nature that appealed to children. The drawings could come from life – leaves, eggs, flowers – or from the imagination – storms, under-sea scenes, rain forests. In the first case, children need examples from nature around them, many easily found in the grounds of most schools. This poem can be found in many anthologies, including Heaney and Hughes (1982) and Sedgwick (2000).

- 'The Tyger' by William Blake. This is widely anthologised; most readily, it is in the indispensable *The Rattle Bag* (Heaney and Hughes 1982).

Drawing inspired by close observation of parts of the children's own bodies

I don't know why I didn't try this idea at Bealings until the last minute. There is no space for the children's drawings here, but they wrote vividly on them:

The more you put your feet up, the more your bones show. My nails are like igloos. My toes are like spoons (Rosemary). The smaller the toe is, the smaller the bone is. Some of my wrinkles are really faint. They are like blinds (Alistair). My nails are like rainbows in an arch. My feet in a shoe feel like they are in a sauna (Anna).

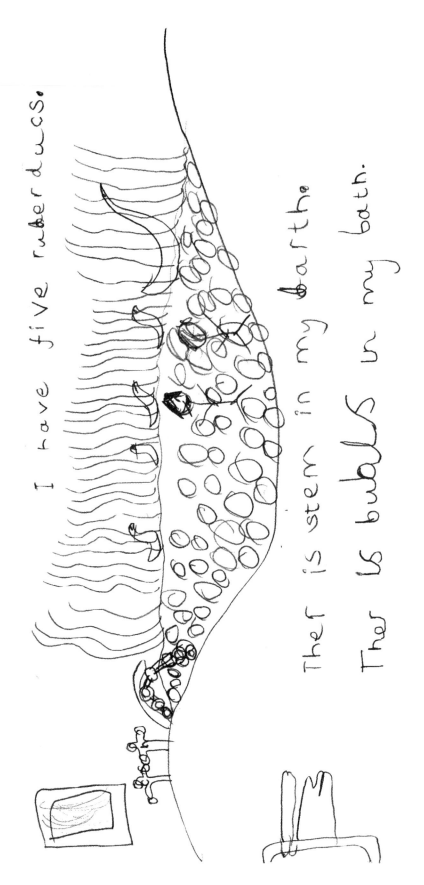

6.2

6.3

In another school, children wrote:

The sole reminds me of an arched bridge. It feels rough, like bricks. The lines on the sole look like pencil scribbles. The heel feels like a fist clenched together. It looks like a hardened nose. It reminds me of clay in a mould and looks like a finger gone numb. The toes look like a mountain going into the distance. They look like cold baked beans.

An impossible place

This title speaks for itself. I ask children to draw an ideal house, with sky, animals, or whatever they want in it. Here is Olivia's piece using this idea (Figure 6.4). Her verbal imagination is fired as well as her visual one. She writes about 'Raining chocolate and candy floss trees and an angel fish. There are balls filled with caramel, and ever-changing secret passageways. People can clamber through the tube and never know where they will come out!' Henry wrote on his drawing: 'The bar supplies cocktails all day. The jercusy (*sic*) is lovely and relaxing.' Jeremy's building was surrounded by 'mountains to stop people getting in'.

Drawing as a preparation for using other media

Drawing is useful as a preparation, especially painting. Often drawing is a maquette (preliminary sketch) for a painting. But note here that, as Read (1931) writes, 'drawing is a distinct art'.

Drawing a story

We all tell stories and we all listen to them – they are a central part of our family life. Here is the beginning of a suggested fiction that might be useful in a drawing lesson. The children should be asked to draw all the time the story is being told, and only stop when the story ends, if it does:

A girl with long wild curly hair walks in a forest. Above her she senses nothing but darkness. She comes across a house made of huge leaves and flowers, the shape of which you have never seen before. The roof seems to be made of tree bark. Through dark, swirling clouds, she sees a weak sun. Out of the tree trunks strides a gross creature that combines all the different animals the girl knows: the fur of a cat, the claws of a bear, the neck of a giraffe, the trunk of an elephant. She runs, her hair flying behind her. Then she turns. Stands bravely. Faces the creature …

Teachers should write their own stories, emphasising visual images, and ask children to draw as the stories are being told.

6.4

Drawing while listening to music

Suggested music, all readily available:

- Bach – Brandenburg Concertos
- Holst – Mars, from *The Planets* suite
- Louis Armstrong – *Potato Head Blues*

The children will suggest music from their own culture that will work well.

Viewfinders

For me, viewfinders need be no more than pieces of card cut to produce a rectangle that can be placed over a part of a subject to be drawn. They change the way of looking by taking the emphasis away from the shape of an object, and by putting it on the texture. And, as Bartel (2000) says: 'viewfinders can simplify the task by isolating the important parts of the subject being observed.' They also help children to 'make choices' and these choices help children to learn, 'the principles of design and composition'.

These children were members of a group of eight- to eleven-year-olds at Gislingham Primary School in Suffolk (Figures 6.5 and 6.6). They used viewfinders to look at parts of the subjects of their drawings. I had taught them my four rules of drawing (p. 14) and also got them to play with the scraps of paper (p. 16). I asked them to draw the borders of the viewfinder before they drew what they could see inside it. Alex's drawing (Figure 6.6), which took 45 minutes to complete, depicts the fabric surface of a musical shaker. It is 'only a bit' of the shaker, he notes. He probably wants to make this clear because he is unused to drawing something without drawing the outer shape first. Kieren's drawing (Figure 6.5) was done as he looked carefully at a part of an electric fan isolated by a rectangle of card. This exercise seemed to cause some distress. Indeed, several of the children called their drawing 'rubbish'. This was because they were being asked to do something unfamiliar. But both the close examination of parts of objects, and the occasional distress, are parts of the lives of artists.

Part 2

Some tentative conclusions

All writing, like all drawing, like all writing worth the name is learning. To take the last point first, if I had arrived at this late stage in this book without the conviction that I had changed, I'd be worried. I do not write to express truths, but to learn them. As W. H. Auden wrote: 'How can I tell what I think till I see what I say?' Serious writers do not write with the conviction that they know something, but with the conviction that there is something to be known, and that by writing, they will come

This is a fane.
This is a fane fan
I am very proud of my self

It looks like the sun rising.

6.5

This is a shaker, only a bit.

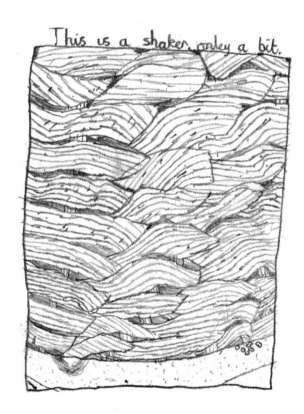

6.6

closer to knowing it. Writers who write merely to amuse or thrill or persuade need not detain us here. I am writing (and I don't care how lofty this sounds) about writers who see writing as like teaching – and therefore like learning.

Back to the classroom. We should judge everything that anyone does in schools not only in terms of what the children are learning, but also in terms of what the adults around them – teachers, learning support assistants, governors, visiting writers and artists, parents – are learning. But our focus is inevitably on the children: those who drew the first sets of pictures of the faces and the cats casually, and who then drew the second sets with a new intensity, have learned more about looking. When the children looked at the African carvings encouraged by the four rules, they learned more about drawing and about line; but they also, even more importantly, learned about the way a people different from their own saw the human figure. When they looked at everyday objects – shoes, plants, climbing frame – they learned that to study such things, to pay them attention, was to learn about attention and looking itself.

And what have I learned? Through the whole project, from April to October, I have learned to trust children's looking more. Sophie's memories of the playground alone taught me this. I have also learned, again, that I am not so much concerned with the subjects of the children's drawings as with their ways of seeing. Perhaps there is no such thing as a dull subject for drawing if the teacher teaches the children to look at it, gives them ways of seeing, and techniques and equipment to record that seeing. Some subjects – a cat moving slyly in the garden, anger at a brother or sister's injustice, leaves and petals swaying on a hollyhock in front of a Victorian brick wall, a carving from Nigeria, a friend's smiling face – are more obviously amenable to powerful drawing than a radiator, say, or a fire extinguisher. But now I know that even the most ordinary things can be made interesting by intensive looking, intensive drawing. A pile of old PE shoes is transformed from an eyesore into art once we look at it and draw it.

I have reinforced an old belief. It can be best expressed in the words of the critic John Berger (quoted in Newland and Rubens 1983:9): 'We never look at just one thing; we are always looking at the relationship between things and ourselves ... seeing ... establishes our place in the surrounding world.' Drawing is a part of education, along with poetry and dance, that enables children (and the rest of us, if we are brave enough) to find a rocky place on which to stand amid the uncertainties of life, among the family, among friends and among the increasing worries of the wider world. Robert Frost wrote that poetry was 'a temporary stay against confusion', and the same is true of drawing.

There is evidence in this book that some children – Olivia, Sophie and Lindsay are three examples – have been feeling their own way, consciously or unconsciously, towards personal statements in drawing for years. They seemed to me to be secure in their drawing, in their visual relationship to the world, when we began on our work for this book. Olivia builds methodically. Sophie and Emily dive into learning as soon as they pick up their pencils. Lindsay and Jonathan also hit the ground running, too, with styles of their own already established. Anna, a teacher's delight, listens, and does what she is told. On the other hand, Henry, assured both socially and between the posts, seems less confident in his drawing. I have seen Henry grow as a draughtsman. We glimpse children's characters in the way they draw. They have begun to develop their own techniques that stem in part from those characters.

But those techniques grow from something else, too. Even these independent youngsters can be more intensely engaged by purposeful teaching: by a good structure that is made up of equipment and encouragement, and the right demands and questions. All children (including those labelled in various ways: special needs, autistic, etc.) can be enabled to learn through drawing by being asked to focus on unusual aspects of a subject; by being asked to see it as though they have never seen it before, as though they were Martians; by looking at something (and, by extension, the universe) from a strange angle. In his drawing of the climbing frame, Henry worked well because I had asked him to concentrate on the spaces between things, rather than the things themselves. This makes the climbing frame, for the time being, unfamiliar; in a literal sense, estranged.

If we make the ordinary extraordinary at the outset, it will lead to art. De-familiarise things, estrange them and then ask children to draw them. For example, turning bicycles upside down makes children look harder at them, and results in drawings that are more accurate, more engaged, more rewarding both for the artist and the viewer. Picking elements out of an object with viewfinders for special attention also has this effect.

Sentences that I have used and overheard that encourage this fresh looking:

- Look at the different shapes you can see in the reflection in the tin, or the spoon, or the crumpled foil.
- Look at the shapes you can see in the animal – the cat, for example – the patterns and texture in its fur.
- Look at the shapes and patterns in the pylon that we can see from the classroom window.
- Look at the darks and lights we can see in that group of objects placed in a big deep box and lit by a torch.
- Look at the pattern and texture on that shell, that stone, that leaf.
- Look at the shapes in that collection of things from the garage, or at the engine of the car.
- How will you tell the person looking at your drawing what that material (the wickerwork of a musical shaker, the fur on a cat's back, the hardness of bricks) feels like?
- How can you make your friend's hair look lifelike?
- Look at his ears. Her eyes. What do they remind you of?

Each of these demands (and hundreds like them) links an element of art to a way of seeing something. The teacher sees and triggers the children to see as well. But sometimes children see before the teacher does, and more intensely than the teacher. This is a lesson worth relearning every time we teach. I can see this in many of the drawings in this book: all the second group cats (pp. 25–9), for example; and Alex's wicker drawing (p. 107).

I learned that it was a mistake to find a lesson taught by an expert and to then think you can teach it without much thought and preparation. I made this mistake with the lesson described based on feeling objects rather than seeing them. The results I achieved were much less interesting than Andrea Durrant's, from whom the idea for the lesson came. When I think about this, I feel guilty: I was not treating the children fairly. Teaching is an art. You have to make its techniques partly your own by reflection before you can make them fully your own by practice.

A note about the 'I can't draw' feeling

I can't draw. I nearly included in the introduction of this book a sketch of the fish in the Pileta caves, done from memory and a postcard, but I thought better of it. I must also admit that I can't dance, in spite of photographic evidence from my summer holiday in Lesvos last year; but that was a Greek dancing night fuelled by ouzo and retsina – and besides, the research student from Edinburgh has forgotten. And I can't sing. (I can't swim, either, but that's probably another story.) And the most shaming admission, among all these shaming admissions, is that I cannot accept anyone saying to me that they cannot write. Everyone can write! Tell me about the last thing your father said to you, or about how you felt when you held your first child in your arms. Remind me of your first Christmas. Write a letter of application for a job. Of course you can write.

I am fully aware of a contradiction here, of course. I have heard choirs of 'can't sing' singers singing – in tune. I once learned to sing in tune myself. This story is relevant to the main argument of this book, which is about looking hard. I *listened* hard, almost until it hurt, to the rondo movement of Tchaikovsky's violin concerto. I was doing this to answer an essay question in an Open University course. We had been asked to count how many times the rondo tune ('Thank GOD it's over, thank GOD it's over') reappears. I lay on the floor of my little flat, listening to the record on my old Dansette record player. For weeks afterwards, I could sing in tune in assembly, even alongside the voices of children – notoriously difficult for unmusical men – because I had trained my ear. The message is clear: we can all be taught to draw, to sing, to write. I only insist on the last one for obvious reasons. That is my obsession. I could learn to draw and dance and sing as well if I wanted to enough. We all could. I have heard teachers saying to children who have complained that their drawings are 'rubbish': 'Don't worry – I can't draw either.' This is a seriously unprofessional remark, no better than 'Don't worry, I can't read.' A teacher taught me once that I couldn't draw, and he taught me this lesson so well that I have never forgotten it. I could name him. Another teacher in the same south London grammar school taught me that I couldn't sing (I could name him too). Yet another taught me that I was no good at maths (Yup). This is all to say that we have monstrous powers as teachers. We can teach children not to be able to do things as much as we can teach them to do them.

We would help children in their drawing if we all behaved as draughtsmen in the classroom, rather than as people frightened of looking foolish when we pick up a pencil. The same is true about writing, dancing and singing alongside children.

A note about graphic tools

Children should use as wide a variety of graphic tools as possible, especially pen and ink. Most schools do not possess enough conventional graphic tools. Some of the tools on the following list were available, but I didn't use them. Here is what I would call a basic list. I have limited the children to black and white because this helps them to concentrate on graphic qualities. Meaning is often 'obliterated' (Newland and Rubens 1983) by colour, especially when the facile question 'Can I colour it in?' is still common in a school.

- Pencils from 6H to 6B
- Charcoal pencils
- Graphite sticks
- Chalk
- Charcoal
- Pens: ballpoint, ink
- Brushes

After experimenting with all these and other graphic tools, it is worth asking children to experiment with other things: twigs, scraps of cardboard, torn-off bits of egg box, screwed-up paper. If we see the tools themselves as teachers, an entire new world of possibilities opens up. Also, children should be given more choice in the paper they use. I was impressed by one school where the children had a choice of colour and size of paper even for writing. For drawing, it is fine to use the cheapest paper sometimes, providing that at other times children can use the best cartridge paper.

Children should be taught to question the suitability of certain graphic tools to certain papers. I have seen children using pencil crayons on cheap shiny paper, or a 6H pencil on huge sugar paper, or powder paint combined with large brushes on A4 paper. It had not occurred to the teacher how frustrating it is to try to make a clear image, let alone a vigorous one, when the tool and the paper don't work together.

Winter is here and the book is finished, or at least abandoned. Outside it is dark at six o'clock. I recall last spring, and my first date with these children at Bealings with pleasure. I hope that they, and Duncan and his staff feel the same. Much has happened. Some of them have gone to secondary school. All of them have learned, either in spite of what we have taught them or because of it. And I have learned that teaching is a job that anyone would do if they really cared about the world and the people who live in it.

I have learned, too, with greater certainty than before, that art teaches us to question everything – our own nature, the way the world works, and our own relationships with that world. The increasingly centralist thinking that rests like a cloud on our schools today sets no store by such questioning. That thinking is concerned with the importance of its own answers. We must resist it. We must enable our children to be like the hidden human beings in the Pileta caves, like Leonardo da Vinci, like Barbara Hepworth. We must help them to assert their humanity in the face of obstacles – we are more than mere ticks on a checklist, or scores on an OFSTED report. We are better than that.

References

Auden, W. H. (1971) *A Commonplace Book*. London: Faber and Faber.

Bartel, M. (2000) 'Helping children learn how to learn how to draw'. http://www.goshen.edu/art/ed/westv.html

Causley, C. (1996) *Collected Poems for Children*. London: Macmillan.

Clayton, M. (1992) *Leonardo da Vinci: the Anatomy of Man*. London: Little, Brown.

Curtis, P. and Wilkinson, A. G. (1994) *Barbara Hepworth: A Retrospective*. London: The Tate Gallery.

Dixon, P. (undated) *Display in the Primary School*. Winchester: Peter Dixon.

Edwards, B. (1992) *Drawing on the Right Side of the Brain*. London: HarperCollins.

Franck, F. (1973) *The Zen of Seeing*. New York: Alfred A. Knopf.

Heaney, S. and Hughes, T. (eds) (1982) *The Rattle Bag*. London: Faber and Faber.

Hepworth, B. (1985) *Barbara Hepworth: A Pictorial Autobiography*. London: The Tate Gallery.

Hill, G. (trans.) (1978) *Brand* by Henrik Ibsen. London: Heinemann.

Kettle's Yard (1995) *Kettle's Yard and its Artists*. Cambridge: Kettle's Yard.

MacKay, D. (1969) *A Flock of Words*. London: Bodley Head.

Mathe, J. (1980) *Leonardo's Inventions*. Geneva: Miller Graphics.

Milne, W. S. (1998) *An Introduction to Geoffrey Hill*. London: Bellew.

Mitchell, A. (ed.) (1993) *The Orchard Book of Poems*. London: Orchard.

Morgan, M. (ed.) (1988) *Art 4–11: Art in the Early Years of Schooling*. Oxford: Blackwell (in association with Suffolk County Council).

National Examinations and Assessment Board (NEAB) (1998) *NEAB Anthology: English, English Literature*. London: Heinemann.

Newland, M. and Rubens, M. (1983) *Some Functions of Art in the Primary School*. London: Inner London Education Authority.

Paine, S. (ed.) (1981) *Six Children Draw*. London: Academic Press.

Pirrie, J. (1987) *On Common Ground: A Programme for Teaching Poetry*. London: Hodder and Stoughton.

Read, H. (1931) *The Meaning of Art*. London: Faber and Faber.

Renner, R. G. (1990) *Edward Hopper 1882–1967: Transformation of the Real*. Cologne: Taschen.

Richter, I. A. (1980) *The Notebooks of Leonardo da Vinci*. Oxford: Oxford University Press.

Sedgwick, D. and Sedgwick, F. (1993) *Drawing to Learn*. London: Hodder and Stoughton.

Sedgwick, F. (1988) 'When you have the feeling', *Times Educational Supplement* 24 June, p. 23.

Sedgwick, F. (1989) *Here Comes the Assembly Man: a year in the life of a primary school*. Basingstoke: Falmer Press.

Sedgwick, F. (1991) *Lies*. Liverpool: Headland.

Sedgwick, F. (1997) *Read My Mind: Young Children, Poetry and Learning*. London: Routledge.

Sedgwick, F. (1999) *Shakespeare and the Young Writer*. London: Routledge.

Sedgwick, F. (2000) *Jenny Kissed Me*. Birmingham: Questions.

Sedgwick, F. (2001) *Teaching Literacy: a Creative Approach*. London: Continuum.

Sedgwick, F. (ed.) (2002) *Will there Really be a Morning?: Life. A Guide*. London: David Fulton Publishers.

Silverstein, S. (1974) *Where the Sidewalk Ends*. London: Cape.

Silverstein, S. (1982) *A Light in the Attic*. London: Cape.

Smith, S. (1975) *Collected Poems of Stevie Smith*. London: Allen Lane.

Stephens, K. (1994) *Learning Through Art and Artefacts*. London: Hodder and Stoughton.

Further Reading

Other books relevant to teaching drawing: a select list

Note: the books of artists' drawings, especially those by Picasso and Giacometti, are recommended because study of them can liberate children from limited views of what drawing can do. The other books in this list have something to offer anyone interested in children's learning through drawing.

Barnes, R. (1987) *Teaching Art to Young Children*. London: Allen and Unwin.

Boudaille, G. (1986) *The Drawings of Picasso*. London: Hamlyn.

Cooke, G., Griffin, D. and Cox, M. (1998) *Teaching Young Children to Draw*. London: Falmer Press.

Cox, M. (1997) *Drawings of People by the Under-5s*. London: Falmer Press.

Giacometti, A. (1984) *The Last Two Decades*. Norwich: Sainsbury Centre for the Visual Arts.

Glimscher, A. and Glimscher, E. (1986) *Je Suis le Cahier: The Sketchbooks of Picasso*. London: Royal Academy of Arts.

Klee, P. (1961) *Pedagogical Sketchbook* (ed. J. Spiller). New York: Wittenborn.

Ocvirk, O. G. *et al.* (1994) *Art Fundamentals: Theory and Practice*. Madison, Wis: Brown and Benchmark.

Read, H. (1943) *Education Through Art*. London: Faber and Faber.

Riddell, B. (1982) *Art in the Making*. London: Evans.

Rogers, M. (1993) *Master Drawings from the National Portrait Gallery*. London: National Portrait Gallery.

Rowswell, G. (1983) *Teaching Art in Primary Schools: A development through activities*. London: Bell and Hyman.

Sedgwick, D. and Sedgwick, F. (1996) *Art Across the Curriculum*. London: Hodder and Stoughton.

Sujo, G. (1994) *Drawing on these Shores: A View of British Drawing and its Affinities*. Preston: Harris Museum and Art Gallery.

Wiltshire, S. (1991) *Floating Cities* (with a Foreword by Dr Oliver Sacks). New York: Summit.